THE BIDEN SCHOOL

AND THE ENGAGED

UNIVERSITY

OF DELAWARE

THE BIDEN SCHOOL AND THE ENGAGED UNIVERSITY OF DELAWARE

1961–2021

DANIEL RICH

UNIVERSITY OF DELAWARE PRESS

NEWARK, DELAWARE

ISBN 978-1-64453-295-9 (paperback)
ISBN 978-1-64453-296-6 (hardcover)
ISBN 978-1-64453-297-3 (epub)
ISBN 978-1-64453-298-0 (web PDF)

Cataloging-in-Publication data is available from the Library of Congress.

A British Cataloging-in-Publication record is available from the British Library.

♾ The paper used in this publication meets the requirements of the American National Standard for Information Sciences—Permanence of Paper for Printed Library Materials, ANSI Z39.48-1992.

Composed in Mercury and Gotham (Hoefler & Co., 1996 and 2000)
Book design by Robert L. Wiser, Silver Spring, MD

udpress.udel.edu

Distributed worldwide by Rutgers University Press

Printed and bound by CPI Group (UK) Ltd, Croydon, CR0 4YY

Frontispiece. Joe Biden at the naming of the Joseph R. Biden, Jr. School of Public Policy and Administration, December 11, 2018. © Kathy F. Atkinson/University of Delaware, all rights reserved.

This book is dedicated to the faculty, staff, students, alumni, and friends of the Joseph R. Biden, Jr. School of Public Policy and Administration—past, present, and future.

CONTENTS

ACKNOWLEDGMENTS

MANY COLLEAGUES generously provided reflections on their experiences at the Biden School for this book. I thank them for their contributions and hope that I have accurately captured their roles in the story. Timothy Barnekov offered numerous suggestions that significantly improved the manuscript. Jeffrey Raffel provided significant insights, and his memoir, *Lessons Learned*, offers an excellent account of his experience as director of the School of Urban Affairs and Public Policy. I received valuable input from David Ames. Maria Aristigueta provided advice and encouragement throughout the project.

Jerome Lewis, Edward Ratledge, and Arno (Skip) Loessner were with the Biden School almost from the start and helped shape its development. They provided critical insights into the school's history, particularly its formative periods. John Byrne, Steven Peuquet, Chandra Reedy, Francis Tannian, Leland Ware, and Danilo Yanich shared recollections of their experiences. Joseph Pika and Ralph Begleiter provided information on initial proposals for a Biden Institute. Nicole Quinn has been a continuing source of assistance throughout the project; she assembled much of the data on the later development of the school. Sebastian Jannelli was an enthusiastic supporter of this project and a source of sound advice on the manuscript and its publication. Catherine McLaughlin provided insights on the Biden Institute. I also thank my colleagues at University of Delaware University Archives and Records Management, Ian Janssen and Lisa Gensel, who provided valuable assistance in obtaining documents from the early period of the school's development. Crystal Nielsen and Kate Dempsey Pfister provided critical help with photographs. Sarah Pragg offered suggestions on manuscript preparation. Laure Ergin provided valuable information on university policies regarding political activity and their relevance to the 2020 presidential campaign.

Some of the individuals important to the development of this book are no longer alive. I especially wish to express appreciation for the work of the late Mary Helen Callahan, who chronicled the accomplishments of the Biden School in the first decades of its development. William Boyer sent me a personal reflection on the development of the MPA program not long before he died. Robert Warren and I wrote together about urban affairs, and many of the thoughts I share about that field were formed by working with him. Robert Wilson died shortly after sending me reflections on his experiences working in the Division of Urban Affairs.

I thank my colleagues and students who have helped me understand the challenges and opportunities facing the University of Delaware and higher education.

I am grateful to Julia Oestreich, the University of Delaware Press director, who provided excellent editorial advice.

My wife Nancy read countless drafts of the manuscript. Her critical eye has made this book better. Any shortcomings are likely the result of not following her advice. Nancy is the one true constant in my life, without whom I could never have taken this journey.

FOREWORD

IT WAS THE SPRING OF 2019 and I found myself sitting in the wood-paneled study of then-former Vice President Joe Biden. We were discussing his prospective run for the presidency, his agenda, and the team he would build around him. As I listened to Vice President Biden talk, I looked over his shoulder and saw a picture of my friend, his late son Beau. Gazing at Beau, dressed in a bomber jacket with a warm smile and the same conviction of optimism in his eyes so many Delawareans had come to know, I couldn't help but think of all he meant to our state and the inspiration he now provided for his father. I looked into Joe Biden's eyes as he spoke about his desire to "save the soul of the nation." And I knew then that he was the man meant for this moment.

It wasn't just my personal connection with Joe Biden that made me believe that he was the person best suited to become the 46th President of the United States. It was his long and distinguished career of public service, underpinned by an understanding of and passion for public policy first inspired and cultivated at the University of Delaware. It was a passion I shared—and one I was similarly privileged to grow at our beloved alma mater when I studied at the school that now bears his name, the Joseph R. Biden, Jr. School of Public Policy and Administration.

My career in public service began decidedly differently than President Biden's did, however. It was an improbable journey—one that would, decades later, lead me to become the first woman and the first person of color to represent Delaware in Congress. And it was a journey aided, in no small part, by the University of Delaware. Rather than rocketing directly to the U.S. Senate at the age of 29, I had spent my twenties traveling the world while going to school and raising a young child. When I returned to the United States, and as I was looking to kickstart my career, I attended a town hall hosted by Delaware's young third-term congressman, Tom Carper. Congressman Carper told me as I had a baby on my hip and one in my womb that his office had internships available. I worked my way up from an intern to a caseworker, where I saw firsthand the government services created through policies, and helped Delawareans navigate those service systems. Through that experience, I gained invaluable insight into which policies were working and which weren't. That's when I began working on designing policy myself, first in the federal government through Congressman Carper's office, and eventually at the state level when I joined him in the Governor's Office.

In the 1990s, I served on Governor Carper's staff as a policy advisor and head of the Family Services Cabinet Council. I was then recruited to join Delaware's largest cabinet agency and became deputy secretary of the Delaware Department of Health and Social Services. Finally, I became Delaware's Secretary of Labor to help connect people in our state to good jobs and spur economic growth. In all of these public service positions, I saw the results of the Biden

School's work. The school is a vital asset to the state, providing both research and technical assistance to inform public decisions and a stream of highly motivated and well-prepared graduates to serve in state and local government and the nonprofit sector.

Having seen the benefit of the school's work throughout my career, I enrolled in its Master's in Urban Affairs and Public Policy program, where I sought to gain knowledge and skills to support me in fulfilling my public service responsibilities. I also wanted to expand my horizons and understand how Delaware's challenges fit with what was happening in the wider world. As a graduate student, I learned the value of research and analysis, translating policy from paper to the real world. As I later described to University of Delaware graduate students, these foundations are more relevant today than at any other time in history. Our research informs practice as much as practice informs research. What we learn as citizen scholars matters to the world.

Earning my master's degree was not easy. By this time, I was a single mom raising two young children and, like other mid-career, non-traditional students, I found it a challenge to balance family, work, and education. I would not have succeeded in earning my degree in 2002 without the assistance of many people at the university, like Raheemah Jabbar-Bey and Karen Curtis, who supported me on my journey.

When I earned my degree, I was state personnel director. That role enabled me to recognize how much the Biden School contributed to the professionalization of Delaware's public sector. The school's graduates were employed in or working with every state agency and virtually all local governments. In addition to its degree programs, the school also offers leadership training programs for staff working in government agencies and nonprofit institutions.

In 2004, I transitioned to the nonprofit sector, becoming CEO of the Metropolitan Wilmington Urban League (MWUL). In this new community-based advocacy position, I observed the Biden School's efforts in addressing Wilmington's growing challenges, particularly those experienced by under-resourced and predominantly Black and Hispanic families. The league actively partnered with the school and its centers on initiatives to increase social equity and improve the quality of life for people of color.

Through my subsequent work in countries around the world like Jordan and China, I came to more fully appreciate the global interconnectedness reflected in public policy and how the research and work being done by the Biden School and its partners has consequences the world over. The school truly seeks to address complex global challenges by employing an open, interdisciplinary lens and to help translate research and analysis into policies and services. The Biden School practices the scholarship of engagement, and it does so at all scales, local to global.

After I was elected to the U.S. Congress in 2016, I appreciated even more the importance of civic engagement for the practice of democracy. I am glad that more Americans from more diverse backgrounds are now involved in crafting public policy, voting, and running for office. At the same time, we have been reminded that our democracy is fragile. That became especially clear to me when I was trapped in the gallery of the House of Representatives on January 6, 2021.

Promoting active citizen engagement in policy-making and governance is central to the Biden School. Its programs range from helping under-resourced communities develop revitalization plans to providing political decision-makers with data and analysis to inform the creation of policies. The school's academic and community programs embody a commitment to public service and a recognition that civic engagement and civil discourse are the lifeblood of democracy. The Democracy Project, for example, is a program for which I've had the pleasure of presenting many times. It is designed to help teachers understand how government works and how their students can become more engaged citizens.

I believe that civic engagement holds the key to preserving our constitutional democracy. We need performers, not spectators. Preparing new generations of citizen scholars and community leaders is what the Biden School is all about.

The history of the school is the subject of this book. It is a story that should matter not only to those who have been and will be part of the school's history but also to those who want to understand how universities can innovate in ways that help address our nation's challenges. I should note that I can think of no one more qualified and capable of writing about this history, himself being a central pillar of it, than Dan Rich. Anyone involved or invested in public policy in Delaware has undoubtedly crossed Dan's path and has been better for it. His affable nature, encyclopedic knowledge, and giving spirit have benefited generations of Biden School students and faculty alike.

The school's story is a model of how universities can make a difference. It is hard to overstate the importance of its contributions to the state of Delaware, helping to drive the professionalization of the public and nonprofit sectors, providing data and analysis that underpin policy, and most of all, producing a diverse group of graduates who are dedicated to public service.

The Biden School's story is still being written. Future chapters will build upon the strong foundations documented here by Dan Rich, and the school will become an even more outstanding exemplar of applying knowledge to address our nation's challenges. As a Blue Hen, I hold as a point of personal pride that our great university produced a president of the United States. But perhaps even more exciting—the school that now bears his name is poised to produce thousands of public servants and citizens who will help us build a better and brighter tomorrow.

Lisa Blunt Rochester
United States Congresswoman, Delaware
July 2022

BIDEN SCHOOL TIMELINE

DIVISION OF URBAN AFFAIRS

1961

Ford Foundation Grant awarded for the establishment of an experimental University of Delaware program in urban affairs.

1963

Census and Data System, which became the Center for Applied Demography and Survey Research (CADSR), established.

1972

Urban Agent Program, which became the Center for Community Research and Service (CCRS), established.

1972

MA and PhD in Urban Affairs and Public Policy created.

1973

Delaware Public Administration Institute, which became the Institute for Public Administration (IPA), established.

COLLEGE OF URBAN AFFAIRS AND PUBLIC POLICY

1976

Master of Public Administration (MPA) created.

1984

Center for Historic Architecture and Engineering, which became the Center for Historic Architecture and Design (CHAD), established.

1984

Center for Energy and Urban Policy Research, which became the Center for Energy and Environmental Policy (CEEP), established.

1997

Masters and PhD in Energy and Environmental Policy (ENEP) created.

SCHOOL OF URBAN AFFAIRS AND PUBLIC POLICY

1997

School joins the College of Human Services, Education and Public Policy.

2005

BS in Leadership transfers to the school, becomes the BS in Organizational and Community Leadership (LEAD).

2009

BS in Energy and Environmental Policy (ENEP) created.

2010

BA in Public Policy, and first accelerated, combined BA and master's program, created.

2010

MS and PhD in Disaster Science and Management (DISA) created.

SCHOOL OF PUBLIC POLICY AND ADMINISTRATION

2011
School joins the College of Arts and Sciences.
2017
Biden Institute founded.
2018
Master of Public Policy (MPP) created.

JOSEPH R. BIDEN, JR.
SCHOOL OF PUBLIC POLICY AND ADMINISTRATION

2018
School named for former Vice President and UD alumnus Joseph R. Biden, Jr.
2019
Master of Public Health (MPH) created with the College of Health Sciences.
2019
PhD in Engineering and Public Policy created with the College of Engineering.
2020
Biden School becomes a freestanding professional school.
2021
PhD in Urban Affairs and Public Policy renamed PhD in Public Policy and Administration.
2021
PhD in Education and Social Policy created with College of Education and Human Development and Department of Sociology and Criminal Justice.

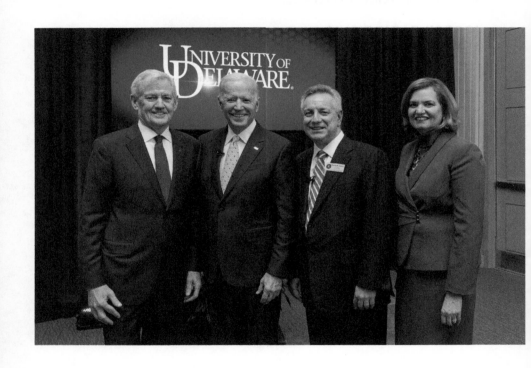

FIGURE 1. John Cochran (left), Joe Biden, Dennis Assanis, and Maria Aristigueta at the naming of the Joseph R. Biden, Jr. School of Public Policy and Administration, December 11, 2018.

INTRODUCTION

ON TUESDAY, DECEMBER 11, 2018, at the semiannual meeting of the University of Delaware Board of Trustees, President Dennis Assanis announced the establishment of the Joseph R. Biden, Jr. School of Public Policy and Administration (the Biden School). The announcement reflected the close, productive, and long-standing relationship between the forty-seventh Vice President of the United States and the University of Delaware (UD). Biden earned his bachelor's degree at the university in 1965 and was a dedicated Blue Hen throughout his public life. During his thirty-six-year tenure as a U.S. Senator, he frequently visited the campus, giving speeches on critical issues, including a passionate address to the university community after the 9/11 terrorist attack. Biden delivered four commencement addresses (1978, 1987, 2004, and 2014) and received an honorary doctoral degree from UD in 2004. In 2012, the university became the repository for his senatorial papers.

FIGURE 2. Joseph R. Biden, Jr., 1965 Blue Hen Yearbook.

There also were strong ties between the Biden family and the university. Biden's wife, Dr. Jill Biden, received an undergraduate degree from UD in 1975 and earned her doctoral degree in educational leadership from the university in 2006. Biden's sister, Valerie Biden Owens, was UD's 1965 homecoming queen and graduated as a dean's scholar in 1967.

Even before Biden was elected vice president, there were many proposals for how the university should recognize and celebrate its most distinguished alumnus. Once he completed his vice presidency, given the recognition that Biden had already received from the university, it was not obvious what further recognition of his public service would be most meaningful.

Shortly after Dennis Assanis was appointed University of Delaware president on November 18, 2015, he concluded that the best tribute to the former vice president, with the most lasting impact on the university's future, would be to add Biden's name to the School of Public Policy and Administration. The school was already a nationally recognized comprehensive school of

1

public affairs, and naming it for the vice president would affirm the school as a priority for the university. "This is an exciting time for public policy education at the University of Delaware," Assanis explained. "By naming our school the Biden School, we not only recognize and honor our most esteemed alum in public service, but we also reinforce our commitment to elevating our school's academic excellence and stature to be among the very best public policy programs in the nation."[1]

A white paper commissioned by Assanis concluded that naming the school for Biden would help propel it to the nation's top tier of public affairs programs.[2] It also would reaffirm the school's historical mission of addressing some of the nation's critical challenges. For more than half a century, the university programs that became the Biden School had carried out this mission. Naming the school signaled the priority of supporting that mission and extending the school's contributions.

HISTORY OF THE BIDEN SCHOOL

This book reviews the history of the Joseph R. Biden, Jr. School of Public Policy and Administration from 1961 to 2021. The focus is on the school's accomplishments over its first sixty years, how they were achieved, and why they are significant. The analysis describes the challenges and opportunities that shaped the school's development and its emergence as one of the nation's leading public affairs schools.

The book is organized into three parts, representing key periods in the school's sixty-year history. Part I chronicles the school's early history from the founding of the Division of Urban Affairs in 1961 through the two decades (1976–96) when it was the College of Urban Affairs and Public Policy. In this period, key programs of applied research and public service were developed, and the *Delaware Model* of public affairs graduate education was created and refined. Part II describes a period of transformation between 1997 and 2014. A college merger in 1997 led to a new designation as the School of Urban Affairs and Public Policy, a unit within a larger, newly amalgamated college. During this period, the school's programs and identity broadened, including the addition of undergraduate programs, and it became a comprehensive school of public affairs. Part III focuses on the period between 2015 and 2021. This period was marked by rising expectations driven by a new vision of the school's development as a pillar of the university.

Each period was characterized by distinctive achievements, many of which were cumulative and influenced the school's long-term development. The Division of Urban Affairs, created through a Ford Foundation grant in 1961 to address the emerging problems of urban America, embodied a new model of university public service and applied research. Between 1961 and 1975, the division developed innovative, community-focused centers that generated and used research-based knowledge to inform public policy. While the initial focus was on Wilmington and the surrounding metropolitan region, the scope of the division's contributions rapidly expanded across the state of Delaware. The programs developed by the division in the 1960s and 1970s became part of the core infrastructure underpinning the school's development over the next half-century.

The creation of the College of Urban Affairs and Public Policy in 1976 represented a critical decision to establish one of the nation's first colleges focused on urban and policy issues. Like the Division of Urban Affairs from which it evolved, the new college was different by design. It was a graduate college in a predominantly undergraduate institution. It was also an interdisciplinary unit carrying out applied research and public service in a university primarily organized around established disciplines and traditional forms of scholarship. The college advocated for greater racial, ethnic, and international diversity in its student body and faculty before university policy fully reflected those values. It accomplished its mission using a unique model of faculty responsibilities, a non-departmental structure, a reliance on centers and institutes to carry out much of its mission, and an innovative budgeting system. These attributes were a source of the college's creativity and, in some regards, enhanced its longer-term contributions to the university.

The college's interdisciplinary, community-focused, and policy-oriented scholarship was pathbreaking, helping to create the field of urban affairs and positioning the various iterations of the Biden School to serve for decades as the professional hub for programs in that field. The school's graduate programs focused on developing a new generation of scholars capable of identifying creative solutions to community problems and translating those solutions into public policies and community services. By the 1990s, the college was carrying out projects with hundreds of local, state, national, and global partners. These collaborations helped to modernize and professionalize Delaware state and local government, improve the performance of nonprofit and community organizations, and strengthen the delivery of public services in domains as diverse as land-use planning and community health, and the provision of social programs for children, families, and neighborhoods. The college brought data, analysis, and professional expertise to governmental decision-making, influencing public policy on issues ranging from educational equity to energy conservation.

The college's research and public service programs and its network of community partnerships supported the development of a distinctive model of public affairs education. The *Delaware Model* enabled graduate students to work alongside faculty and professional staff to apply what they learned in their classrooms to concrete public policy challenges. The model has gained special recognition in the field of public administration because it integrates theory and practice in ways not typical of most public administration programs. When the school later offered undergraduate programs, those students also benefited from the *Delaware Model*, having access to experiential learning opportunities usually available only to graduate students.

In 1997, when the college became the School of Urban Affairs and Public Policy, it joined a new larger college created to increase the impact of university programs in the community. The following decade was notable for the expanding scope of the University of Delaware's engagement in public issues. In many ways, UD became an exemplar of an *engaged university*, an institution organized to use knowledge to enrich the overall quality of life in the communities it serves. During the 1990s and early 2000s, aspirations for the school focused more explicitly on it becoming a comprehensive school of public affairs. Early in the twenty-first century, it ranked in the top tier of such schools.

In 2011, the school changed its name to the School of Public Policy and Administration to better reflect its broadened scope. After a reorganization, it joined the College of Arts and Sciences. The Great Recession of 2008 and the complications of the school's changing institutional location resulted in a contraction of resources. Even so, when the school celebrated its fiftieth anniversary, its impacts on the university, on public affairs education and research, and on communities across Delaware were well-documented. Many of the school's earlier graduates had risen to leadership positions in public and nonprofit institutions, while others carried out scholarship on critical policy issues.

In 2015, President Assanis announced a new vision of the school's role in the university's overall development. That vision included naming the school for then-Vice President Biden. After the vision was announced, the school expanded. The faculty grew from 24 in 2015 to 35 in 2019.[3] The number of Biden School graduate students also increased, reaching an enrollment of 200 in fall 2021.[4] Another essential step followed in 2020 when the Biden School of Public Policy and Administration became the first freestanding professional school at the university, placing it on an institutional level comparable to the nation's other leading public affairs schools. As of this book's writing, the school offers five doctoral programs, six master's programs, three undergraduate majors, and four undergraduate minors. It has six research and public service centers, including three core units created a half-century earlier. It also includes the Biden Institute, for which Joe Biden was the founding chair.

The Biden School's history is instructive beyond its importance to those who have been part of the school or benefited from its research and public service programs. The school has been an innovator in its organization and curricula. Throughout its history, the school has faced demands to become more aligned with traditional academic structure and norms. At several points, the future of the school was at risk. In each case, the school prevailed. The history of the school is thus a story of institutional innovation, perseverance, adaptation, and resilience.

The Biden School's journey also provides a case study of organizational leadership in higher education. Most studies of higher education leadership describe the contributions of one or a few university leaders, typically in a single period in an institution's history. The Biden School has engaged many leaders within the school and the university over more than a half-century. The school's directors and deans, and center and academic program leaders, some of whom served for decades, have made key leadership contributions. Equally important, intellectual and creative leadership from faculty and staff has generated new approaches to public affairs education and research and a comprehensive, novel model of university public service. The Biden School's long-term success was also made possible by critical commitments from university administrators at key points in its history. Without those commitments, the school might not have survived, much less thrived. The history of the school chronicles the influence of many types of leaders and forms of higher education leadership over more than half a century.

The Biden School has always engaged in "translational research," using the knowledge it generates to address the wider community's challenges, bridging the world of ideas and the world of action. What began in 1961 as an experimental program supported by a single external grant emerged six decades later as one of the nation's leading comprehensive schools of public affairs. That transformation unfolded during one of the most dynamic periods in the history of higher education, when the public purpose of universities was debated and eventually expanded.

THE PUBLIC PURPOSE

The Biden School's history is deeply intertwined with the University of Delaware's emergence as one of the nation's premier engaged research universities. Over more than half a century, the school expanded UD's public purpose. That purpose is reflected in the university's mission, which describes it as "an institution engaged in addressing the critical needs of the state, the nation, and global community."[5]

Founded in 1743, the university expanded its mission when it became a land-grant institution. When the Morrill Act of 1862 was enacted, the United States was still predominantly a rural and agricultural nation. The legislation ceded federal lands to states with the provision that proceeds from selling that land would fund collegiate programs in such "useful arts" as agriculture, mechanics, mining, and military instruction. In addition, the "land-grant" funding would "promote the liberal and practical education of the industrial classes in the several pursuits and professions in life."[6] The 1862 law granted Delaware an allocation of ninety thousand acres of federal land. The funds from selling that land created an endowment for Delaware College, which later became the University of Delaware.

The university, which had been struggling financially, "was not only saved by financial support from the Land Grant Act but given a mission of public service that would bind it to the people of our State forever."[7] The land-grant designation marked the beginning of its dual public/private identity, which remains a crucial part of its institutional character. While becoming the flagship public university of the state of Delaware, the University of Delaware retained features of its initial status as a private institution, most notably in its governance by a self-selecting board of trustees.

For most of the hundred years after the Morrill Act went into effect, the land-grant identity of the university centered on its programs in agriculture and engineering, then known as the mechanical arts.[8] The provision of the Morrill Act to expand education to "the industrial classes" (such as factory workers) had little impact. When it became a land-grant institution, the students served were white men, 75 percent of whom came from Delaware. The Women's College was not established until 1914. The University of Delaware was a racially segregated institution. The second Morrill Act in 1890 led to the establishment of Delaware State College (later Delaware State University), a land-grant institution for African Americans that shared in the land-grant resources that came to the state. UD remained segregated until a ruling by Judge Collins Seitz in the case of *Parker v. University of Delaware* in the Delaware Court of Chancery eliminated formal segregation in 1950.[9]

Most land-grant colleges and universities, including the University of Delaware, were modest-sized institutions until after World War II. Following the war, U.S. higher education underwent a dramatic expansion driven by a redefined public purpose. Government leaders proclaimed higher education as the pathway for millions of citizens to join a prosperous middle class and believed that a college-educated labor force is essential to U.S. economic prosperity and national security. Federal and state investment fueled the rapid expansion of colleges and universities.[10] John Thelin calls the period from 1945 to 1970 "higher education's golden age."[11] One of the key drivers of this growth was the Servicemen's Readjustment Act of 1944 (popularly known as the G.I. Bill). The legislation enabled returning veterans to pursue higher education rather than enter the postwar labor market. The result was a remarkable growth in enrollments at colleges and universities.[12] In 1939–40, UD reached its highest prewar enrollment of 939 students. Right after the war, in 1946–47, the number doubled to about 1,900; nearly two-thirds of those students were returning veterans.[13] Student enrollments at the university continued to grow for the next seventy years, reaching over twenty-four thousand in 2020.

The federal government also expanded the public purpose of universities through investment in research and advanced graduate and professional programs. In the decades after World War II, universities were viewed as having a central role in helping to solve critical social and economic challenges—ranging from the Cold War to the War on Poverty. National security was the core argument driving the ramp-up of federal funding for research and development. Recognizing that the mobilization of university scientists and engineers could help win the Cold War, federal government leaders expected that those scholars should be relied upon to help preserve the peace. Universities accordingly invested in programs, research facilities, and infrastructure to attract federal funding. Annual federal funding of research and development at institutions of higher education doubled from $9 billion to $18 billion between 1970 and 1990. It almost doubled again to $32 billion by 2008, with much of this investment going to a concentrated group of research universities, which Clark Kerr called "federal grant universities."[14]

The University of Delaware became a major research university later than many state flagship institutions. Through the 1990s, most of its externally funded research was in a few science and engineering departments or units that received funds because of the university's designation as a land-grant, sea-grant, space-grant, and, for a short while, urban-grant institution. UD remained a predominantly undergraduate institution with limited externally funded research activity. There was a strong tradition of engaging undergraduates in research at UD because there were few graduate students with whom research-oriented faculty could work. There was also a relatively modest externally funded research program to support graduate students. Graduate programs did not expand significantly until the 1960s and 1970s, and even at the start of the 1990s, the university's full-time graduate enrollment was still barely more than 1,500. From the 1960s through the 1990s, UD's investments in expanding its research and graduate profile were highly selective, focusing on areas that were likely to gain the university national prominence. The creation and expansion of the programs that would become the Biden School were a product of that selectivity. However, the initial impetus for these programs was much more than the opportunity to gain prominence in an academic field.

The programs were also a response to an external invitation to address the growing challenges of the nation's cities and do so by bringing together scholars from many disciplines to work directly with the communities to be served. The Biden School's beginnings reflected UD's decision to become a more engaged university, one committed to interdisciplinary, action-oriented scholarship. From the outset, the Biden School represented an expansion of UD's public purpose. That expansion continued, helping the University of Delaware become one of the nation's most engaged research universities during the first sixty years of the school's history.

PART I

CREATING THE
DELAWARE MODEL
(1961–1996)

FIGURE 3. Wilmington, during the 1968 unrest.

CHAPTER ONE

THE DIVISION
OF URBAN AFFAIRS

THE BIDEN SCHOOL evolved from the Division of Urban Affairs, established in 1961 to address the challenges facing urban America, specifically those in Wilmington, Delaware, and the surrounding metropolitan region. The forces that gave rise to the University of Delaware program and other university-based urban affairs programs are complex and unusual compared to those behind the creation of traditional university programs. Most of the pressure to establish urban affairs programs came from outside the academic community rather than from scholars working on urban issues.

By the 1960s, many older cities were experiencing an unprecedented outmigration of population and businesses to new and growing suburbs. Poverty became increasingly concentrated in central cities, which were suffering declining economic investment and job opportunities, and faced with diminishing resources to tackle their challenges. The U.S. War on Poverty, driven by President Lyndon Johnson's Great Society initiative, reaffirmed the urgency of meeting domestic challenges, many of which were in America's cities. During the 1960s and 1970s, the federal government invested massive funds for "solution-oriented" training, research, and services related to creating, operating, and evaluating a vast number of federally spawned urban projects. Governments, private institutions, and community organizations called upon universities to play a more active role in their communities and mobilize their resources to help alleviate the poverty, racism, institutional disorder, and environmental blight that threatened the nation's cities and menaced its residents.

THE FORD FOUNDATION CHALLENGE GRANT

The first investments in urban affairs programs came from the Ford Foundation rather than from state or federal government. Between 1959 and 1974, the Ford Foundation distributed $36 million in start-up grants that challenged U.S. universities to establish new programs designed to address the problems of urban America.[1] The foundation's challenge embodied a double-edged critique of the prevailing approaches to these problems at U.S. universities. First, urban challenges did not come neatly bundled along the disciplinary lines that defined the academic organization of traditional university faculties.

The issues of housing, transportation, inequality, and segregation did not fit within the boundaries of separate disciplines like political science, economics, sociology, law, planning, or psychology. The Ford Foundation focused its competitive grants on creating new interdisciplinary programs. The federal government later affirmed in its grant programs that the traditional disciplinary organization of universities was ill-suited to address the practical challenges facing the nation's communities.

Second, the foundation insisted that often-insular universities reach out to those living and working in urban communities to understand the nature of the problems those populations were experiencing. To do this, universities needed to place people and expertise in the communities they were serving. The approach underpinning the original urban affairs programs was to bring together scholars from diverse fields, organize them outside the traditional university structure, and give them a mandate and funding to carry out applied scholarship on community problems. These programs were to become a bridge between the university and the community. The responsibility of their faculty and students was to move across that bridge in both directions. The measure of their success would not be scholarly citations but community impacts and improvements.

On September 20, 1960, UD President John Perkins submitted a proposal to the Ford Foundation to "establish a permanent program of urban services within the University of Delaware." The proposal stated that the "compactness and rapid urbanization of the State of Delaware, the current absence of organized concern about problems of urbanization and the central role of the university in the life of the state, combine to create an unusual opportunity for a program of urban services." The proposed university program of extension, research, and education would "translate and expand the land-grant college approach so successful in the rural setting to the urban setting which predominated in our State and times." The program would develop over five years, involve many parts of the university, seek to involve citizens and organizations, and "provide assistance to public officials and governments." The communities of the state would be utilized "as laboratories and classrooms in which to learn about and to help meet problems of urbanization."[2]

The proposal described a three-part program that would be university-wide and interdisciplinary, creating a modernly conceived urban extension service, establishing a related research program on urban problems in Delaware, and introducing new educational activities relevant to the urban field. The program director would appoint "field agents" from various disciplines who would work in a manner parallel to agricultural extension agents and carry out research and extension services in the community. The proposal pledged that the program developed under the grant would become a permanent feature of the university.[3]

On April 20, 1961, Perkins received a letter confirming that the Ford Foundation awarded the University of Delaware a $500,000 grant for the proposed program.[4] As confirmed in the award letter, the program would "include an urban extension service to the community, a complementary research program, a modest educational and training program consisting of noncredit institutes and seminars for public officials and interested citizens, and an expansion of pertinent credit course offerings in appropriate colleges of the university."[5]

In some respects, the University of Delaware was an unusual choice for one of the first Ford Foundation grants. In 1961, the university was still a modest-sized institution located in a small city with a population of fewer than thirty thousand people. A regionally focused university, its undergraduate enrollment of 3,600 was made up mainly of Delawareans. It had few graduate programs and only 340 full-time graduate students, most of whom were in the sciences and engineering.[6] The university also had limited research capacity in the social sciences, with most of that research conducted by individual scholars for publication in journals and books, not for community application. The faculty had minimal experience carrying out grants or contracts with restrictions and targeted requirements.

In other ways, the University of Delaware was a perfect choice for a new interdisciplinary program intended to bring expertise to bear on the challenges facing America's urban communities. UD was a land-grant university, and the Ford grant supported programs that would operate in urban areas in ways that paralleled land-grant programs that had served rural America throughout the previous century. At the time, UD was also in a formative period of developing new programs, some of which cut across traditional academic units. Further, the city of Wilmington manifested all the interconnected and growing problems of urban America: poverty, racism, crime, inadequate housing, environmental blight, inefficient planning, and overburdened and under-professionalized government programs.

The Division of Urban Affairs was created to carry out the Ford Foundation grant requirements, and Edward Overman was appointed as director. Overman had worked in government research at the University of Virginia and the University of Tennessee before joining UD, where he held a faculty appointment in the Department of Political Science.[7] The division was "situated in the structure of the University in a manner calculated to emphasize its role in activities external to the University."[8] It reported to Vice President for University Relations George Worrilow.[9] At its inception, Worrilow defined the path for the future when he recognized that the grant made it possible for the university to form a special kind of unit. The initial professional staff hired in the division had diverse social science and planning backgrounds. They would work in teams to address the multifaceted problems of Delaware's communities. Quite intentionally, the division represented a mid-twentieth-century reinvention of the nineteenth-century land-grant concept, now focused on addressing the emerging demands of an increasingly urbanized society.[10]

Yet, the new program represented more than the translation of a century-old idea to emerging conditions. It also expressed the university's commitment to improving conditions in the state's most distressed communities—those experiencing the most significant challenges. In Delaware, that meant a focus on the city of Wilmington.

WILMINGTON'S WOES

In the 1960s and 1970s, Wilmington faced challenges that mirrored those of much of the rest of urban America but with some features unique to the city's and the state's political and economic environment. In 1960, Wilmington, with a population of ninety-six thousand, was Delaware's largest city and had been the hub of its economic growth through the first half of the twentieth century. Dubbed the corporate capital by UD historian Carol Hoffecker, Wilmington was the headquarters of the DuPont company.[11] The mark of the company and the historical influence of the du Pont family were present in and around the city in everything from its architecture, housing, and cultural amenities to the spawning of a diverse array of legal and other service institutions that supported the global center of the chemical industry. Because of its corporate identity and investments in commercial buildings and support services, Wilmington had a core infrastructure suitable for a much larger population.

Without question, the DuPont company brought prosperity and notoriety to the tiny state of Delaware.[12] There was a significant relationship between the economic success of DuPont and the economic vitality of the state, particularly Wilmington. Many in Wilmington prospered from DuPont's growth. However, the distribution of benefits did not reach all of the city's population, specifically low-income Black families. After World War II, conditions in the city began to change dramatically. Parallel to the pattern familiar in so many other U.S. cities, Wilmington's population began to drop while surrounding New Castle County grew. From 1940 to 1970, the city's population declined by nearly 30 percent, while the county's population increased by over 100 percent.[13] The exodus from Wilmington was no accident. Much of it was driven by public policy. As summarized by William Boyer, "government policies were killing the city. Wilmington's drop in population was exacerbated in the early 1960s by I-95's emasculation of the city. The city was eviscerated, too, in the early 1960s when twenty-two square blocks of east side residences—including both good and dilapidated housing—were lost to urban renewal, scattering the working-class families with negative results."[14] As a result of these changes, many middle- and upper-income residents left the city. Many businesses followed, "leaving a depleted downtown, with no movie theaters and only two supermarkets in the city. In the meantime, the city became increasingly populated by blacks and the poor."[15]

The concentration of African Americans and other minorities was also a product of housing discrimination that excluded them from living in much of the surrounding area of the county.[16] As the more affluent left the city, they took their tax dollars, leaving fewer resources available for city services.[17] Wilmington was left with a high concentration of Black and low-income families and declining employment opportunities for unskilled labor, while the suburbs continued to grow and prosper.[18] Given the dominant role of DuPont in Wilmington, it is not surprising that the leadership to address these challenges came from Henry B. du Pont, who guided the establishment of the Greater Wilmington Development Council (GWDC) to support the revitalization of Wilmington and the surrounding areas. Understanding the GWDC is essential for understanding the environment within which the Division of Urban Affairs worked. In its first years, the division entered into several contracts for research with the GWDC.

The GWDC wielded a great deal of political influence at the state and local levels, and it used that influence both formally and informally to promote its agenda. In 1967, it sought legislation to eliminate discriminatory housing practices because industries in the Greater Wilmington area were having trouble recruiting Black professionals to move to the city. The GWDC was not entirely business-focused, however. In the late 1960s, the organization provided funding for neighborhood service centers, sponsored an analysis of education resources in Wilmington, and advocated for a community college to be opened in the center city. Working with the Division of Urban Affairs, the GWDC promoted the professionalization of public service employees and was influential in establishing the first staff of professional planners in Wilmington.[19] In these respects, the council acted as a form of private government for Wilmington, often eclipsing formal government institutions in delivering expanded programs and services to support a new path for development.[20]

The GWDC partnered with the Division of Urban Affairs to study the state and regional economies, how they were changing because of urbanization, the shifting locations of businesses and employment within the region, and the implications of these changes for Wilmington's central business district.[21] With financial support from the GWDC, the division launched "a program of research into the dynamics of the economies of the region."[22] The alliance of the division staff with private sector leaders focused on the emerging factors influencing economic development in the city and across the state. The division's research also looked at consumer attitudes about shopping and living in Wilmington and the broader policy environment affecting the economy, including tax policies. "It is believed," Overman proposed, "that the Division of Urban Affairs has made one of the most complete and valid analysis of personal income ever made for a whole state."[23]

The critical event that impacted Wilmington's development in this period occurred in 1968. The unrest within the Black community in the wake of the assassination of Martin Luther King, Jr., led then-Delaware Governor

Charles Terry to declare a state of emergency and order the National Guard to occupy the city. The details of the events that precipitated that occupation are subject to debate, but what is not debatable is that after the unrest was over, the governor refused to withdraw the National Guard. He continued to refuse despite the pleas of local business leaders, political leaders, and city residents.

Joe Biden, who returned to Delaware in the summer of 1968 after graduating from law school, found Downtown Wilmington a "strange place." He walked to work past soldiers carrying rifles every day: "Apparently they were there to protect me." Biden elaborated on the different community responses to the National Guard's presence:

The white citizens the TV reporters interviewed were almost all happy to have the Guard there. They were afraid riots might ignite in the ghetto and then spread from there. They were afraid Wilmington's police force wasn't big enough to keep it contained. Generally, they were afraid.

But in the black neighborhoods of East Wilmington, residents were afraid, too. Every evening National Guardsmen were prowling their streets with loaded weapons. Curfews were in effect from dusk to dawn. Mothers were terrified that their children would make one bad mistake and end up dead. The locals called the nightly National Guard reconnaissance rounds "rat patrols." "They patrol our streets like we're animals," black citizens would say. "They take away our pride."[24]

The experience had a profound influence on Biden. He knew that "blacks and whites weren't talking to one another." He also knew that "white residents of Wilmington had no idea why black residents of the city complained about the way" Governor Terry and the National Guard were treating them. Did they have the same constitutional protections and freedom of movement as those living in white neighborhoods? Biden continued, "I thought the folks in those neighborhoods deserved at least that much. I didn't think I could change the world in 1968 or even what was happening, but I thought I could make a difference. So I walked across Rodney Square and into the basement of a three-story building and applied for work in the public defender's office."[25]

Biden's walk across Rodney Square started a public service career that began with his election to the New Castle County Council in 1970. That experience further heightened his recognition of the mounting challenges in Wilmington, particularly for its Black and increasingly low-income population. As Carol Hoffecker has pointed out, the riots of April 1968 represented the "nadir of Wilmington's postwar decline."[26] The National Guard remained in Wilmington for nine months, the longest military occupation of an American city since the Civil War, until Terry was defeated at the polls by Russell Peterson, a DuPont chemist. Peterson's first act as governor was to remove the National Guard. The occupation was stigmatizing for Wilmington and further accelerated the city's downturn. Property values dropped,

FIGURE 4. National Guard Occupation of Wilmington, 1968.

FIGURE 5. National Guard Occupation of Wilmington, 1968.

and the pace at which population, businesses, and jobs left the city increased. Wilmington became smaller and poorer, with shrinking public resources to support city services.

In the 1970s, competition between Wilmington and the surrounding areas of New Castle County increased and pitted suburban residents against those living in Wilmington. As Hoffecker explains, "The most important public issues in Greater Wilmington during the 1970s, inter-district busing, metropolitan government, and the future location of the area's major hospital, all pitted the interests of the city against those of county residents."[27] Increasingly over the next two decades, policy decisions on these and other issues often further disadvantaged the city. Given the lack of progress for twenty years in implementing the Supreme Court's *Brown v. Board of Education* decision (which included two Delaware cases), the federal courts mandated metropolitan school desegregation in 1974. This court decision resulted in the elimination of the Wilmington School District and ten other New Castle County districts and introduced countywide busing of students.[28] Faculty and staff from the Division of Urban Affairs researched shifting demographic patterns and policies affecting school desegregation and the public attitudes about these changes. They also chronicled the politics of the metropolitan school desegregation process and its impacts.[29] For the next half-century, faculty, staff, and students from the programs that eventually became the Biden School remained engaged in analyzing public education policy impacting Wilmington and educational equity across Delaware.

The conditions in Wilmington in the decades after World War II paralleled those of cities across America. The corporate center of the city continued to prosper. However, those who worked in the corporate center increasingly lived in the suburbs, and those who remained in the city were unable to leave. At its scale, Wilmington's challenges were as acute as in any city in the nation. It also seemed to observers, including some at the Ford Foundation, that if those challenges could not be solved in the small city of Wilmington, then there was little hope to tackle them in New York, Chicago, or Los Angeles.

DEVELOPING THE DIVISION

The Division of Urban Affairs's mandate was to develop research-based knowledge that policymakers could use to address the problems in Wilmington and other Delaware communities. In carrying out this mandate, the division faced challenges of its own. The most immediate was its lack of the data needed to conduct research and analysis. The university had no established social science or policy centers generating data. Overman identified capacity issues as a top priority, pointing to the need to "build a state-wide system of data acquisition, processing, and dissemination geared to the long-range planning and operating needs" of communities and state agencies.[30] Without such capacity, the division and its partners, such as the GWDC and

FIGURE 6. Edward Ratledge, director of the Census and Data System,
with Phyllis Rabb (left) and Judith Molloy (right), 1980.

government agencies, would be unable to effectively pursue objectives such as strengthening the planning capacity of Wilmington and other Delaware communities, evaluating the ongoing changes in the regional economy and their impacts, or documenting the social problems generated from urbanization in and around Delaware.

For the first decade and a half of its existence, the division was building this capacity. At the same time, it was completing studies for government and community institutions, often under contract. The interdisciplinary staff included political scientists, public administration specialists, economists, demographers, and sociologists; most did not have faculty appointments. The staff was more racially diverse than the university staff and student body. It included community development specialists and other practitioners and advocates not in typical academic departments. Notably, the initial senior staff had little background and experience in urban issues. Most had focused on rural issues and now sought to translate their knowledge to an urban setting. The staff also had no experience building community-focused research capacity, yet they were determined to do so.

A critical step in building such capacity was developing a census and data system headquartered at the division but involving many state and local agencies. It was an ambitious effort to draw public planning, transportation, and school agencies "into a state-wide system of data acquisition, processing, and dissemination geared to the long-range planning and operating needs of these agencies."[31] The system also would be used as a research resource for the division and other parts of the university. In 1963, the Census and Data System, which later became the Center for Applied Demography and Survey Research, was formally established to provide current, accurate demographic information and analysis to decision-makers in communities throughout the state.

The Census and Data System conducted interview surveys on prominent policy issues such as school desegregation and the reapportionment of the Delaware General Assembly. It also helped form the Delaware Population Consortium to produce a single set of demographic projections for all governments and informed state decision-makers on policies such as taxation. This work required skills quite different from those of traditional faculty. Edward Ratledge, who joined the division in 1973 and became director of the Census and Data System in 1974,[32] explains that the staff needed "a wide and flexible interdisciplinary research outlook. They also needed to be visible to the policy community and communicate with a broad spectrum of decision-makers. Hence, the need for professional staff and self-selected faculty who would create a different model of engaged scholarship that incorporated public service as a priority."[33] Their projects built on one another, such that the staff learned new skills and acquired additional data systematically. This work also generated valuable off-campus relationships with state leaders that led to "invitations to participate in taskforces, commissions, advisory boards, and other policy advisory positions, most of which were uncompensated public service but opened doors for funded projects."[34]

During its early years, the Division of Urban Affairs focused on leveraging university resources to assist community groups, municipalities, nonprofits, and public agencies throughout Delaware. A key objective was to enhance the planning and policy-making capacity of municipalities and regional and state agencies. In the early 1960s, there was little such professional capacity in Wilmington, New Castle County, or any other community in Delaware. Overman proposed that improving planning capacity was essential for communities to address the problems of urbanization.[35] When the City of Wilmington and other municipalities hired planning professionals, the division acted as a support institution, engaging them on an Inter-agency Planning Committee to coordinate planning efforts. The committee also included representation from the GWDC and state officials. Municipalities throughout the state called upon the division to assist with developing comprehensive plans. In the first two years, it worked on plans for the cities of Newark, Dover, New Castle, Smyrna, and Laurel. Technical assistance in the development and implementation of municipal and county planning quickly became a staple service.

The division also conducted demographic analysis, including a population and housing analysis of the Wilmington metropolitan region. That analysis drew attention to the changing racial backgrounds and income levels of the population in the city and the surrounding suburban parts of New Castle County. The division staff sought to demonstrate to decision-makers and the public that policy analysis and planning mattered. Research on policy and planning issues and options could identify new possibilities for addressing critical community issues.

During its first five years, the division's public service and applied research programs broadened dramatically. Much of this work was supported by external federal and state grants and contracts, as well as by direct support from municipalities. The division launched projects in the areas of educational policy and urban services, community organization and neighborhood development, housing and land use, government organization and municipal administration, and poverty and racial equality. Based on its initial work, the division was one of only two programs that received a supplemental grant from the Ford Foundation in 1966.

G. Arno (Skip) Loessner, appointed assistant director of urban services for the division in 1969, recalls that the responsibilities for evidence-based analysis carried special obligations for division faculty and staff not to participate in partisan politics or engage in private consulting with the State of Delaware.[36] Loessner explains, "The main thing was to be able to back up our work with evidence and maintain recognition for objective analysis."[37] Jeffrey Raffel, hired in 1971, believes that unbiased analysis was the key to the

FIGURE 7. G. Arno Loessner, assistant director of urban services (1977).

impact of the division's work. The division offered more than technical assistance and research capacity; it also provided legitimacy and an appearance of neutrality for consulting policy-makers because "nobody questioned the validity of our results."[38]

The Division of Urban Affairs's capacity-building efforts continued in the early 1970s. In 1972, the Urban Agent Program was created. Later renamed the Center for Community Research and Service, the program was located in Wilmington to provide direct, ongoing research and technical assistance to community institutions, especially in low-income neighborhoods. It formalized the urban agent work underway from the outset of the Ford Foundation grant in which "agents" applied various community organization strategies, including some new models, to cultivate community-based economic development.

With James H. Sills, Jr., as director, the Urban Agent Program was not only in the community, but it also acted on behalf of the community. Sills was a community organizer and a recognized Wilmington leader before joining the University of Delaware. He was the first African American executive director of People's Settlement, a nonprofit social services agency located in Wilmington's Eastside that served the city's immigrant population and subsequently focused on helping the increasing number of poor and Black families. Sills had also served as an at-large member of the Wilmington City Council between 1968 and 1972 and was directly involved with efforts to end the National Guard occupation of the city. When Sills became the head of the Urban Agent Program, he was already widely recognized as a community activist, a political leader of the Black community, and an outspoken advocate for the university to take on a more significant public service role.

FIGURE 8. James H. Sills, Jr, director, Urban Agent Program, and state representative (1974).

Under Sills's direction, the Urban Agent Program became a vehicle for addressing the challenges facing low-income and increasingly Black neighborhoods. This advocacy contrasted with the focus on unbiased assistance that was a cornerstone of the work of other units in the division. The work done by Sills and his colleagues in the program at times entailed challenging major economic institutions, particularly banks whose mortgage and lending practices discriminated against minority and low-income residents.[39]

By the early 1970s, the scope of the division's work encompassed the entire state. Notably, the division staff working with Mayor Crawford Carroll of Dover helped establish the Delaware League of Local Governments in 1970, which operated from the division's offices in Newark.

Loessner defined a three-year program to coordinate services among local governments and improve their recognition and representation in Legislative Hall in Dover. The collaboration with the league continued over the next half-century, primarily through the work of the Delaware Public Administration Institute. In 1973, the institute, which later became the Institute for Public Administration, was established to pursue this broader, statewide effort through partnerships with local, state, and regional governments and public agencies. Jerome Lewis was appointed director, with specific responsibility for supporting the professionalization of those in government agencies at all levels.[40] At the outset, a federal grant program under the Intergovernmental Personnel Act of 1970 focused such services on personnel practices, including assisting with employee selection processes and labor relations. The institute became the home base for the Delaware Association for Public Administration and the Delaware Chapter of the American Society for Public Administration.[41]

FIGURE 9. Jerome Lewis, director, Delaware Public Administration Institute (1978).

Within less than a decade, the Division of Urban Affairs had developed a substantial capacity for applied interdisciplinary research on a wide range of public issues. It also maintained growing collaborations with communities across the state and state agencies. It became "one of the most vibrant, involved and influential institutions in the State of Delaware."[42] At the same time, it remained outside of the established academic structure of the university, reporting to the vice president for university relations rather than to the provost. There were no faculty appointments in the division, although some staff held faculty appointments in the social science departments. It offered no instructional programs and had no students of its own but did establish an Urban Fellows program in 1962. This program enabled students in disciplinary social science master's programs to serve as research assistants for faculty on projects focused on addressing urban challenges.

Throughout its first decade, the internal operations of the division remained informal. Many decisions were being made in an ad hoc manner by the director. While this ad hoc decision-making was not surprising for a new unit outside of the university's academic structure and focused on work for external clients, the second director, C. Harold (Hal) Brown, enhanced this informality with his management style. He often prided himself on not conforming to bureaucratic rules, and had a one-on-one approach to management that relied little on formal policies. Raffel recalls that Brown made decisions without formal staff meetings or any agreed-upon rules, and this adhocracy continued even after the first faculty were hired.[43]

FIGURE 10. C. Harold Brown, director, Division of Urban Affairs, 1968–75; dean, College of Urban Affairs and Public Policy, 1976–78.

Robert Wilson, hired to lead the division's demographic and evaluation research programs once Brown was made director, recalls that the size of the division staff, about twenty in total, was small enough "to fit into the recreation room in Hal and Sally Brown's home."[44]

A NEW MODEL OF UNIVERSITY PUBLIC SERVICE

By the mid-1970s, the division had carried out more than two hundred studies for government and quasi-governmental agencies at various levels and had built a reputation as Delaware's primary source for policy analysis and research on public issues. Not all of its work was in policy analysis and planning, however. Much of the work was on the ground in communities across the state, building partnerships that would serve as the foundation for longer-term improvements in services and policies. Raffel notes that trust was a factor of critical importance for division staff in building those partnerships in a small state and "the foundation for our success in the decades ahead."[45]

The division's success through the mid-1970s was difficult to judge because many of its achieved outcomes were discernable only after a decade or more. Some of the most dramatic results of the division's work were indirect: professionalizing city and county workers, strengthening the capacity of community organizations and public/private partnerships, and improving the data available for public decision-making.

One clear result is that the Division of Urban Affairs changed the University of Delaware. It introduced a new model of university public service guided by applied research on emerging community needs and challenges. To implement this model, the university created an organization different from a typical academic unit. In hindsight, the creation of the division was a crucial step in UD's evolution into an engaged research university. Over the next half-century, the public service and applied research centers developed in the 1960s and early 1970s remained critical components of the future Biden School. The centers were also the foundation for new and distinctive academic programs.

In 1974, a Ford Foundation evaluation of the urban university programs it had supported concluded that most of its funded experiments had been less than effective. It identified the University of Delaware's Division of Urban Affairs as among the few notable successes.[46]

FIGURE 11. David L. Ames, dean, College of Urban Affairs and Public Policy, 1979–89.

CHAPTER TWO

THE COLLEGE OF URBAN AFFAIRS AND PUBLIC POLICY

IN 1975, THE DIVISION OF URBAN AFFAIRS became the secretariat for the Council of University Institutes for Urban Affairs, initially comprised of the directors of urban affairs programs across the nation. Division Director Hal Brown helped create the organization, which became the Urban Affairs Association (UAA) in 1980, to serve as the leading international professional organization for scholars and researchers of urban affairs. Mary Helen Callahan, a professional staff member of the division, provided the central administrative support for the new organization and became the executive director in 1975, serving in that capacity through 2000.[1] The University of Delaware's leadership of the UAA contributed to the division's reputation as one of the nation's model urban affairs programs.

In 1976, the council's national meeting focused on the prospects for the field of urban affairs. With state and federal funding and foundation support, often matched by university investment, urban affairs programs had mushroomed in number from a handful in the 1960s to several hundred by the mid-1970s.[2] However, many of the social forces that gave rise to the field weakened. Proclamations of an urban crisis and strident demands for social justice and equality were replaced by calls from public officials and civic leaders for sounder fiscal management and greater efficiency in municipal services. Some members of the Council of University Institutes for Urban Affairs questioned the future viability of urban affairs programs when they were no longer a political priority and could not pull in the external funding they had attracted earlier. Indeed, any program's prospects seemed to depend on both its self-reliance in generating resources and the continuation of its university administration's support. That was the case for the Division of Urban Affairs.

BECOMING A COLLEGE

The late 1960s and early 1970s were turbulent times on the University of Delaware campus, as they were on many university campuses during the Vietnam War and Civil Rights Movement. At UD, the local chapter of the Students for a Democratic Society (SDS) organized anti-war rallies, challenged UD's compulsory military training—a product of the institution's land-grant heritage—and, in spring 1967, gained leadership positions in the Student Government Association.[3] Led by the SDS and with the support of some faculty, students directly challenged university policies, particularly those related to student conduct. Amidst these turbulent circumstances, on June 10, 1967, UD President John Perkins resigned.

After serving as vice president for academic affairs at the Georgia Institute of Technology, E. Arthur Trabant became president of the University of Delaware on July 1, 1968. In the year since Perkins resigned, Provost John Shirley, who served as acting president, had presided over a campus that remained mired in controversy over student rights. Periodic anti-war protests continued, including a brief sit-in at the university administration building. Another sit-in was held at the student center to bring attention to ongoing civil rights struggles. All of this was happening as the university continued to grow dramatically. Undergraduate enrollment increased from 2,400 in 1957–58 to 6,500 in 1967–68, driven in part by dramatic increases in Delaware's population.[4] As a result, the university added academic programs, faculty, and facilities yearly.

From the outset, Trabant took a very different path from Perkins in charting the next stage of the university's development. He called upon the students, faculty, and administration to create a new "Community Design" for the university's future. He initiated a process headed by a Community Design Commission that engaged all university units in a multi-year process that resulted in the 1971 publication of a strategic plan entitled *The Decade Ahead: The Report of the Community Design Planning Commission*. The two-volume report described guiding principles for the university's growth and included detailed plans prepared by each academic and non-academic unit. UD was predominantly an undergraduate institution, and the report indicated that expanding the university's graduate programs was a clear priority. There was no medical school or law school, nor any likelihood of launching either, given the high costs of doing so.[5] That created the opportunity, indeed the need, for other graduate and professional programs that might help enhance the university's overall profile as a graduate institution.

Even before the strategic plan was completed, the Division of Urban Affairs staff began to design a graduate program. In 1970, the university approved faculty appointments in the division, anticipating that a graduate program would be approved and that the division would then become an academic unit. The Community Design Commission recommended that the division become a graduate college of urban affairs and included a detailed proposal for a new PhD program. As the 1971 report proposed, making the division a college would provide a place where students and faculty could engage in research, education, and service related to the contemporary issues of urban life. Social issues would be the "source and target" of these initiatives, which would "stress the interdependence between basic theory, systematic research, and the application of scientific knowledge to policy and practice."[6]

L. Leon Campbell became provost in 1972, with a clear mandate to carry out the recommendations of the Community Design Commission. His efforts focused on moving UD from an undergraduate institution to a full-scale university with recognized strengths in graduate education and research extending beyond traditional areas of excellence. Campbell concentrated on areas where UD could excel. Two areas selected for priority were marine studies and urban affairs, leading to the creation of the College of Marine Studies and the College of Urban Affairs and Public Policy. Notably, both colleges reflected UD's identity as an engaged university, and both were extensions of its public purpose, especially its land-grant identity.[7] Also notable was that both colleges were established as graduate-only institutions, differentiating them from the university's other colleges, all of which had undergraduate and graduate programs.

The university officially established the College of Urban Affairs and Public Policy in 1976. Public policy was included in the name because the Division of Urban Affairs had already expanded to encompass a broader mission than that of the original unit supported by the Ford Foundation, emerging as a key resource of state and local government for a broad range of policy research and analysis. It also provided technical assistance for the design and delivery of public programs and services. Hal Brown, director of the division, was appointed as dean of the college. Dan Rich, the division's associate director, became associate dean of the college. In 1978, when Brown was appointed UD vice president for employee relations, Rich became acting dean, and the university launched a national search for Brown's successor.

In 1979, David L. Ames, professor of Urban Studies and Planning at Virginia Commonwealth University, was selected to become the college's dean.[8] After he started, he concluded that "the college was even better than I imagined. Hal Brown had systematically developed a superb urban affairs faculty with scholars from urban sectors of several social sciences."[9] The research and public service units had earned national recognition and were emulated by other universities. Moreover, the college had "solved the problem of being responsive to the needs of the community by creating public service faculty positions and supporting them with professional staff," thereby creating the capacity to "respond to needs of the community as they arose and continue to work with them in an ongoing fashion."[10]

AN INNOVATIVE ORGANIZATION

The organization of the College of Urban Affairs and Public Policy was distinctive. Many of the opportunities and challenges the college faced over the next two decades were the direct result of being organized and operated in a manner unlike most academic units. First and foremost, the college was not organized into academic departments. The directors of the new academic programs, the MA and PhD in Urban Affairs and Public Policy and the Master of Public Administration, reported to the associate dean through program committees. While most University of Delaware faculty had nine-month academic year appointments, the college's faculty had twelve-month appointments. These extended appointments were justified because community challenges were continuous, so faculty and students would be participating in engaged scholarship and public service year-round. Also, all the faculty were affiliated with at least one of the college's centers or institutes. They would be partially funded through work conducted with the centers, often supported by external contracts and grants. The centers also employed graduate students as research assistants on externally supported projects supervised by faculty or senior professional staff, some of whom had secondary faculty appointments.

Ames recalls that each research and public service center served a specific constituency in the state. Each had a professional staff with skills related to the work conducted for that constituency. The Census and Data System was the recognized source for population data and projections for state agencies and conducted surveys for governmental and private clients. The Delaware Public Administration Institute was devoted to the planning, management, and service-delivery needs of state and local governments. The Urban Agent Program in Wilmington was concerned with the needs of low-income and disadvantaged communities.[11]

The college also had a unique budgeting system, which granted it greater autonomy than a typical academic unit but required it to generate support from external grants and contracts. For a university with a modest externally funded research imprint at this time, most of which was in the sciences and engineering, this system was a bold step. The new college needed to generate sufficient external funding to support its graduate students, fund professional staff, and cover the cost of its extended faculty appointments. However, in exchange for receiving less funding from the university, the college had the freedom to generate and keep any positive balance at the end of each fiscal year. The college was also given the flexibility to add positions supported by external funds. The budgeting arrangement was a great advantage for the college and provided the incentive structure and flexibility necessary to generate and creatively use resources from diverse sources.

Beyond these organizational factors, the college was substantively different from others in the university because it valued and was designed to support interdisciplinary and applied scholarship and to prepare graduate students to carry out such scholarship. The college's promotion and tenure requirements placed a premium on the integration of research, instruction, and service, and the demonstration of community impact as well as scholarly impact. As promotion dossiers made their way up from the college to the university level, they often looked different from the typical portfolios—and they often were different. As a graduate-only college, its teaching metrics looked different than those for faculty in units with undergraduate programs. Given the college's interdisciplinary makeup, faculty published in a wide variety of outlets, many outside of traditional scholarly publishing networks. The idea of documenting public service and community engagement seemed foreign and often irrelevant to traditional faculty, who often thought of such service as a lesser responsibility and focused on contributions to the university or national professional associations. The university's Faculty Senate did not officially recognize engaged scholarship in its promotion criteria until 2018.

A NEW GENERATION OF URBAN AFFAIRS SCHOLARS

The graduate program in urban affairs and public policy filled a knowledge gap in the social sciences. In the decades after World War II, the traditional social sciences—political science, sociology, economics—became embroiled in controversies about whether and how social inquiry should be more scientific and empirical. While some scholars researched emerging social and economic challenges, most focused on constructing their disciplines. Prodigious scholarly debates about the direction of each discipline arose shortly after the war and continued through subsequent decades.[12] These dialogues were inward-looking, and by the 1960s and 1970s, the leading social science journals were largely barren of any consideration of substantive societal challenges or research-based policy proposals to address them. The result was the increasing isolation of scholarship. It was this, Irving Louis Horowitz pointed out decades later, that set the stage for the emergence of new, interdisciplinary fields of social science, including urban affairs and policy studies.[13]

The College of Urban Affairs and Public Policy's graduate program sought to prepare a new generation of interdisciplinary scholars who would generate usable knowledge to inform public decisions. In retrospect, the search for such knowledge was both idealistic and naive. It focused on creating and using research and analysis to improve communities, but it was unclear how this knowledge could be translated into public policies and programs. Even so, the new graduate program, and others like it across the nation, projected confidence about the power of ideas to guide social action and social change.

Danilo Yanich (PhD, UAPP 1980), who was in one of the college's first cohorts of doctoral students, found the program's orientation to be precisely what he wanted based on his experience as a War on Poverty community organizer. He recounts that he knew very little about the people he was serving as a community organizer other than that they faced different degrees of poverty. He could not effectively advocate for them because he did not understand the forces influencing their lives. Yanich came to the graduate program because he wanted to "reconcile the disconnect between the world as I was experiencing it and the prevailing theories as I knew them. With its design to be different, challenging, and out-of-the-box, the program perfectly suited what I thought was needed in the messy world of social action."[14]

After he graduated, Yanich joined the faculty and remained a part of the various iterations of the Biden School throughout his career. In 2006, he became director of the graduate program in urban affairs and public policy from which he had graduated.

The college matched a focus on urban affairs with the study of public policy and policy analysis. It also addressed the implementation of policy, understood variously as public administration by those with a governmental orientation and as theories and strategies of social change by those more focused on community-based action. Its program connected the interdisciplinary fields of urban affairs, public policy, and public administration. The faculty and students located themselves among these disciplines according to their theoretical orientation or, more often, to what seemed most valuable to their research on housing, education, poverty, service delivery, community and economic development, or the improvement of government programs, policies, and services.

In the early years of the program, there was a great deal of faculty debate and experimentation regarding how to meet objectives, as there were no established graduate programs of this type to serve as models. The program faculty came from specific disciplines, mainly sociology, political science, and economics. While they sought to create a truly interdisciplinary program, each spoke a different disciplinary language and used concepts and methods from their discipline. A continual problem was slipping back into those specific approaches rather than connecting them in new and intellectually productive ways.

The program relied on team-teaching of the core seminars, particularly the doctoral seminars, but it soon became apparent that putting an economist, sociologist, and political scientist together in the same classroom did not necessarily produce interdisciplinary discourse. Jeffrey Raffel describes the challenge: "The Ph.D. program was supposed to be interdisciplinary and to be based on interdisciplinary theories. Unfortunately, we found that whatever we named the courses, we were really teaching in the disciplines we had learned-political science, sociology, and economics."[15] Francis Tannian, an economist and one of the architects of the graduate program, recalls that there was no discussion of "how we would integrate various approaches."[16] In effect, the faculty asked the students to do something that the faculty themselves were largely unable to do.

Over time, the faculty developed more confidence in the program's core structure, which took shape around their areas of research, often conducted in collaboration with the doctoral students. However, one of the issues that remained a challenge throughout the program's development was evaluating the background and qualifications of prospective students.

The college maintained an outspoken commitment to the diversity of its student body in terms of academic background, race, ethnicity, experience, and professional objectives. The faculty also placed less emphasis on some

FIGURE 12A Francis Tannian, professor, 1966–98, and
FIGURE 12B Robert Wilson, professor, 1968–2009.

standard indicators of student qualifications, such as Graduate Record Exam (GRE) scores, than on factors such as motivation and prior experience that were not so tangible. Longtime professor Robert Wilson recalls that the first students were "a remarkable bunch: a former nun, a cab driver, and some idealists who wanted to be urban change agents."[17] In 1976, Clyde Bishop, who

was in the initial group of students, became the first graduate of the PhD in Urban Affairs and Public Policy. A Black Delawarean who received an undergraduate degree from Delaware State University and a master's degree in sociology from UD, Bishop worked in various jobs but could not decide on a career. He recalls that the new graduate program "interested me because it was a unique, interdisciplinary graduate program. It integrated economic, political, and social policy issues, and that made sense to me because it seemed to fit the way things are in the real world."[18] After receiving his doctorate, Bishop went on to a career in academia and the U.S. Foreign Service. In 2007, President George W. Bush appointed him U.S. Ambassador to the Marshall Islands.

FIGURE 13. Clyde Bishop, the first graduate of the PhD in Urban Affairs and Public Policy, at the 1976 UD Commencement with his children.

Enrollments grew throughout the 1980s, with graduate student funding provided primarily through grants and contracts from faculty and professional staff, often working through the college's centers. By the end of the 1980s, the PhD in Urban Affairs and Public Policy program was the largest doctoral program in the social sciences at UD. Its reputation grew as its graduates moved into faculty positions at other institutions and maintained connections with the University of Delaware as alumni and active members of the Urban Affairs Association, the secretariat for which remained at the College of Urban Affairs and Public Policy.[19]

The students entering the PhD program after completing the master's program were typically the best prepared for the demands of doctoral study. The MA in Urban Affairs and Public Policy, first awarded in 1973, was initially a point of entry leading to the PhD program. By the 1980s, however, the master's began to attract more professionally oriented students who wanted a terminal graduate degree that prepared them for practice in planning, community development, nonprofit leadership, or historic preservation. More doctoral students entered the program with master's degrees from other institutions and diverse disciplines. The diversity of student backgrounds and interests translated into a wide range of dissertation topics. Some topics were outside the realm of traditional social science scholarship but of great consequence to the broader community, such as poverty and racial and ethnic equality. The broad scope and varying scholarly content and methods reflected in the dissertations written by the college's students remained a challenge for decades, as there was no consistent rubric for evaluating such diverse work.

In 1984, J. Barry Cullingworth, a senior faculty member and highly productive scholar, reviewed the college's completed dissertations. He concluded that they were amorphous and difficult to conceptualize. Further, the overall faculty capacity in scholarly research was not sufficient in scope to support the diversity of the doctoral dissertations. Ames recalls having a different assessment: "We were in uncharted waters with no disciplinary canon or established research streams. The dissertations addressed issues that had not previously received academic attention. As for the number of people to serve on committees, we reached out throughout the university for dissertation committee members who were very strong."[20]

The urban affairs and public policy graduate program became a bundle of programs wrapped up in a single package. That students attracted to the program had a broad range of social and policy interests could be viewed as a strength, but concerns grew about the resulting challenges. Student research areas ranged widely, including education, social services, energy policy, community development, and public management. Some students were looking for a professional doctoral program, and others were seeking a research degree. While most students were full-time, the program also served part-time students. The result was that the program was subject to increasingly different expectations. There was continuing faculty debate about the types of students in the program, the proper curriculum, the standards students should meet, and the best use of program resources, particularly student funding.

In 1987, an external review team appointed by the UD Faculty Senate to evaluate the program affirmed that it was among the best-known urban affairs programs in the nation.[21] Still, it criticized the program for being too open-ended in the scope of its research and for accommodating students with too broad a range of backgrounds and scholarly interests. It recommended that the doctoral program be better defined to focus on a few established areas of faculty scholarship. The program was subsequently redesigned around specializations that reflected the faculty's primary areas of scholarship: urban governance, planning, and management; technology, environment, and society; and social and urban policy. Ironically, this served to fragment the college's entire program across these broad areas (and their various subfields as defined by the faculty) rather than reunify it around scholarship in the core field of urban affairs or affirm it as a graduate degree program in public policy and policy analysis.

PUBLIC ADMINISTRATION

The University of Delaware had prominent scholars in public administration in the 1950s and 1960s but no established academic or research program. John Perkins was a nationally recognized political scientist specializing in public administration. While serving as University of Delaware president, he was the editor of *Public Administration Review*, the major journal in the field. In addition, the university had an endowed professorship in public administration held by Felix Nigro, chairperson of the Department of Political Science in the late 1960s. In 1969, William W. Boyer succeeded Nigro as department chair and Charles P. Messick Professor of Public Administration.[22] Boyer received a commitment from university administration to start a Master of Public Administration (MPA) program, a step that an outside evaluation group had previously recommended.[23] Soon after his arrival, Boyer concluded that the MPA program should be developed jointly with the College of Urban Affairs and Public Policy: "Within only a few months, I became familiar with the urban affairs program and staff, including Jerome Lewis and his Institute for Public Administration, and research that Skip Loessner and others were doing for Delaware's state and local government. And I came to the conclusion that the only way an MPA could become a reality was for our two units—political science and urban affairs—to offer and administer it jointly. I further concluded that Jerome Lewis should direct the MPA degree."[24] Boyer and Lewis garnered support on campus and from those across the state who would benefit from the program. The program was approved in 1976, and the first MPA degree was awarded in 1978.

While the program was being created, the National Association of Schools of Public Affairs and Administration (NASPAA) adopted a uniform national curriculum and student service quality standards for the accreditation of MPA programs. The Delaware MPA was among the first such programs to align with the new national quality standards. In 1982, NASPAA formally reviewed the Delaware MPA and certified it as meeting the highest standards for such graduate programs, making it one of the first programs in the nation to be certified.[25]

The MPA was designed primarily as a full-time degree program, although it did admit part-time students and subsequently developed a mid-career option. What was distinctive about the MPA program from the outset was that it offered students the opportunity to work alongside the faculty and professional staff of the college on applied public administration projects throughout the state. From the program's inception, the Institute for Public Administration provided ongoing leadership and support both for the program and its students. The role of the Department of Political Science was ultimately limited to a few faculty who taught courses for the program.

By the end of the 1980s, enrollment had grown to sixty students, most of whom were full-time,[26] and the MPA program was well established within the college. The need to meet growing accreditation requirements from NASPAA led to a reorganization of the college's faculty. While still avoiding the creation of separate departments, the college was organized into two separate program faculties, one for urban affairs and public policy and the other for public administration (with cooperation from the Department of

Political Science). All college faculty had a primary designation in one program or the other, and the heads of each of the programs had some duties and responsibilities equivalent to department chairs. This model of separate program faculties and program directors continued when new academic programs were added.

EMERGING DIRECTIONS OF SCHOLARSHIP

The scope and impact of the college's applied policy research and public service often overshadowed its more scholarly contributions, even though the scholarly research productivity of the faculty increased consistently over the 1980s. College faculty and staff increased their output, particularly in several specialty areas, including urban policy, energy and environmental policy, and historic preservation. The growth of work in these areas led to the creation of two new interdisciplinary centers: the Center for Energy and Urban Policy Research (renamed the Center for Energy and Environmental Policy in 1993) and the Center for Historic Architecture and Engineering (renamed the Center for Historic Architecture and Design in 1996).

In 1980, an informal Energy Policy Research Group began to plan for a new center and graduate concentration that would address connections between energy policy and urban policy. Led by John Byrne (PhD, UAPP 1980), the group included faculty members Young-Doo Wang (PhD, UAPP 1980), Dan Rich, and Francis Tannian. Members of the group had researched options to improve energy efficiency and household energy consumption and had worked with the Delaware Public Service Commission to examine a variety of electric utility policies impacting demand and possibilities for conservation. In 1982, the group was awarded a grant from the Unidel Foundation to support the development of interdisciplinary research and graduate education in energy policy. The research program grew rapidly and, in 1986, the Center for Energy and Urban Policy Research (CEUPR) was established, with Byrne as director. CEUPR supported interdisciplinary and collaborative research in energy, environmental, and urban policy, building on the work of the earlier research group. By the end of the 1980s, the center sponsored an area of specialization in the urban affairs and public policy graduate program and was attracting students internationally. In 1989, CEUPR provided financial support for sixteen graduate students who worked with center faculty and staff on research in the U.S. and, increasingly, in other countries.[27]

The second interdisciplinary research initiative focused on historic preservation. A working group led by faculty members David Ames, Bernard Herman, and Rebecca Siders collaborated with Art History, Art Conservation, and Civil and Environmental Engineering researchers. In 1982, the group received a grant from the University of Delaware Research Fund to support students working on documentation of historic resources. Two years later, their research program transformed into the Center for Historic Architecture

FIGURE 14A Robert Warren, professor, 1975–2013, and
FIGURE 14B J. Barry Cullingworth, professor, 1983–94.

and Engineering (CHAE). The center "grew out of a crisis on Delaware's historic landscape in the early 1980s," as rapid development across the state posed severe threats to historic buildings and the preservation of structures with cultural significance.[28] Chandra Reedy, who became director of the center in 2017, recounts the original reason behind its establishment:[29] "The impetus for its founding was an intense threat faced by the historic built environment of northern Delaware from rampant and uncontrolled development in the 1970s and 80s. The initial focus of the Center was on recording information on historic buildings and landscapes prior to their destruction, using measured drawings and photographs."[30] Initial work focused on documenting buildings in Wilmington and New Castle County "with drawings, photographs, and narrative research before they were demolished."[31] Center "faculty and staff quickly began expanding their research along the lines of the rapidly changing historic preservation movement in the United States, developing broader contexts to understand better the ways in which the past shaped the built environment of the mid-Atlantic region."[32] The center's work also expanded to encompass the entire state.

Through a long-term cooperative agreement to document historic resources, CHAE became the first university center recognized by the Historic American Buildings Survey/Historic American Engineering Record.[33] The documentation of historic buildings throughout Delaware became a continuing program of the center, engaging graduate students in the MA in Urban Affairs and Public Policy.[34] The center focused on cultural resource planning and architectural history and documentation.[35]

Both CEUPR and CHAE actively engaged faculty, research professionals, and students from other colleges in their research programs, providing university-wide focal points for interdisciplinary research and graduate education. They broadened the scholarly identity of the college and of the university as a whole.

By 1989, the College of Urban Affairs and Public Policy had several senior faculty with national recognition, particularly in urban affairs. An assessment of urban affairs scholarship ranked Robert Warren among the nation's most cited scholars during the review period of 1986–89. Warren's scholarly reputation attracted a significant number of doctoral students, and he played a central role in the overall development and visibility of the PhD program.[36] The assessment of urban affairs scholarship also recognized J. Barry Cullingworth, one of the nation's leading urban planning scholars.[37] In 1989, the college's faculty and staff published five books, three monographs, twenty-one journal articles, and fifteen technical reports.[38]

GROWING PAINS

Initially housed in two small buildings, Raub Hall and 5 West Main Street, with some offices in Willard Hall and other locations, the College of Urban Affairs and Public Policy moved to Graham Hall on Academy Street in 1984, but not without complications. The pressures of assigning space in Graham Hall added to tensions within the college.[39] In 1985, Timothy Barnekov was appointed associate dean with the explicit responsibility to improve administrative and operational practices and internal communication between the dean's office and the academic program and center leaders.[40] New managerial procedures were introduced, including an improved financial reporting system and more open and systematic communication.

By 1987, the college had fourteen faculty, sixteen professional staff, and twelve support staff.[41] It had forty-eight PhD students, twenty-three MA students, and sixty-eight MPA students. It also had five research and public service centers.[42] While the college was growing in size and reputation, the finances to support its operations did not keep pace. Changes in national and state priorities had shifted away from areas that previously generated external support, particularly those related to poverty, community organization, and social and economic equity. By the late 1980s, fiscal uncertainty became institutionalized as a chronic condition, as the college had no process for sharing resources across centers and programs to better manage the college-wide impact of the changes in external funding.

The growing pains reflected the college's continuing transition and also the fact that the university was changing. Between the 1960s and 1980s, the University of Delaware grew dramatically, doubling undergraduate enrollments from 6,500 in 1967 to 13,000 in 1980, with continued growth through the 1980s.[43] Graduate and research programs expanded, and so did the physical plant. President Trabant and Provost Campbell had led the university throughout that period of growth. In 1987, Trabant retired. Campbell resigned as provost in 1988, shortly after the appointment of Russell Jones as president on July 1, 1987. Jones immediately engaged the entire university in developing a five-year plan called Project Vision, but he never completed the plan. Jones came into conflict with the Board of Trustees, and on October 24, 1988, he announced his resignation. Trabant returned as president while a presidential search got underway. The search resulted in David Roselle becoming UD's new president on May 1, 1990.[44]

FOCUSED PRIORITIES

By the time Roselle became president, the College of Urban Affairs and Public Policy was well-established and nationally recognized for its distinctive graduate programs and applied research and public service. In 1992, a national ranking of U.S. graduate urban affairs programs ranked UD's program fourth in the nation.[45] The MPA program received a six-year reaccreditation from the National Association of Schools of Public Affairs and Administration. The growing number of alumni of the College of Urban Affairs and Public Policy led to the establishment of the United Alumni of Urban Affairs (UAUA), which hosted its first event in 1990 and initiated efforts to support the college and provide educational and professional development opportunities for current students. In 1992, the college awarded its first-ever Distinguished Alumni Award for outstanding achievement to Richard Schneider. A graduate of the U.S. Coast Guard Academy, Schneider earned his PhD in Urban Affairs and Public Policy in 1985 while serving as executive officer of UD's College of Marine Studies (later part of the College of Earth, Ocean and Environment). In 1985, Schneider became vice president for research at Drexel University and later was appointed interim vice president for academic affairs and senior vice president for administration. In 1992, Schneider became president of Norwich University, where he continued to serve as of 2021, one of the longest-serving college presidents in the country.[46]

FIGURE 15. Richard Schneider (PhD, UAPP 1985) received the first Distinguished Alumni Award in 1992.

In 1991, Dan Rich was appointed dean of the college, almost simultaneously with the University of Delaware initiating a series of campus-wide budget reductions. A significant turning point in the development of the college came the following year. Faced with budgetary pressures across campus, Roselle and Provost Byron Pipes called for a review of the college to assess its continued value and cost-effectiveness. A College Review Committee was established by the provost that was chaired by Professor Carol Hoffecker and included other UD faculty members. A key question was how the college fit with the emerging priorities of the university. When Roselle became president, he streamlined his predecessor's unfinished Project Vision strategic planning process and called his new plan Focused Vision. He hoped to project clear priorities for the university's development and expected the colleges to do the same.

The challenge for the College of Urban Affairs and Public Policy was that there was no longer a shared vision for its future development among its faculty and professional staff. As the college grew and added programs and centers, the earlier focus on urban affairs had dissipated. Many faculty and staff worked in public administration, historic preservation, or a specialized policy field such as energy and environmental policy. At the same time, the centers were growing apart. Even within the graduate programs, the scholarly focus was becoming broader and more diffuse, with more faculty and students focused on scholarship in particular areas of specialization.

The College Review Committee cited the college's graduate programs for earning a high national ranking and making significant contributions to the university, both in terms of students' academic qualifications and achievements and the professional accomplishments of graduates. The committee's report also pointed to the college's high-quality public service programs and their importance to state and local government. Notably, the report drew attention to the cost-effectiveness of these functions and the synergy of public service, research, and graduate education, "the chief accomplishment of the college," deserving of continuing university support.[47] Recommending that the college remain an exclusively graduate degree-granting unit with a greater focus in areas of strength, the committee also encouraged the engagement of undergraduates in the college's public service projects. It urged the college to become even more proactive in focusing on the most critical urban, social, and policy issues and bringing the expertise of faculty and students throughout the university to bear on addressing these issues.

The committee's report became the springboard for a strategic plan that aligned the College of Urban Affairs and Public Policy's development with university priorities. The central premise of the plan was that the college needed a stronger scholarly and intellectual center of gravity to underpin its graduate programs and a stronger alignment of those programs with its research and public service centers. In line with the plan, the MPA program faculty redesigned all areas of specialization. The Delaware Public Administration Institute was formally designated to provide direct support for students in that program. The MA also was modified to create a terminal professional degree track. Its program faculty approved new concentrations in areas that the college's centers could support: community analysis and development, and nonprofit leadership (Center for Community Development); energy and environmental policy (Center for Energy and Environmental Policy); and historic preservation and planning (Center for Historic Architecture and Engineering).[48] Similarly, the doctoral program further concentrated on a few areas of research: urban governance and planning; technology and society, with a focus on energy and environmental policy; and social policy, with a focus on education and health policy and community development. It began to focus on admitting students planning to study in those specific areas.

Overall, the college became more self-reliant, especially regarding its finances. Despite budget reductions from the university and increasing competition for external funding, the college carried positive balances between 1991 and 1995.[49] It built a reserve account for salaries to provide start-up funding for new projects and carryover funding for professional staff between grants. It also established a reserve account for graduate student funding, enabling admissions committees to make early funding commitments to new students.[50] A new overhead policy returned 50 percent of the college's overhead to its units with the expectation that they would build up their reserves and rely less on the college for unplanned expenses. These changes encouraged the college's growth through the 1990s.

CHAPTER THREE

POLICY PARTNERSHIPS
AND THE *DELAWARE MODEL*

THROUGHOUT THE 1980S AND 1990S, the College of Urban Affairs and Public Policy developed partnerships with public and nonprofit institutions to collect and analyze information, evaluate policies and their alternatives, develop management systems, plan for future needs, and train managers and community officials. While most partner institutions were in Delaware, a growing number were national and international. Predominantly supported through the college's centers, these partnerships represented an extensive network of clients and collaborators.

By the end of the 1980s, the college was annually serving 150 public, private, and nonprofit agencies.[1] That number increased through the 1990s. As of 1992, in addition to state and local organizations, clients included fifteen foreign or international organizations, sixteen federal government agencies, and four national nonprofit organizations.[2] The broadening intellectual scope of scholarship in the college engaged some of the emerging state, national, and international challenges in energy and environmental policy, historic preservation, and urban economic development. By 1995, the number of program partners annually served by the college increased to over two hundred.[3]

As the number of partnerships grew, so did the staff of the college's centers. Some staff members were recent graduates from the college's academic programs, and others were established professionals with experience and specialized skills in applied research and analysis. By the end of the 1980s, there were more research and public service professionals in the college than faculty members. The number of faculty members was increasing, although more slowly than the number of professional staff. New faculty were encouraged to have extended contracts that included appointments in the centers intended to support external contracts and grants.[4]

Graduate students served as research assistants on virtually all partnership projects. The research assistantships funded their education and enabled them to work alongside faculty and professional staff applying what they learned in the classroom to actual policy, planning, and administrative challenges. These funding and experiential learning opportunities attracted an increasing number of graduate students through the 1980s and early 1990s.

Between 1991 and 1995, graduate student financial support more than tripled, reaching $1.6 million; the number of funded students increased from forty-two to ninety-two. Virtually all of the increased funding came from college-generated sources, including an increase in externally sponsored research and public service from $1.5 million in 1991 to $3.5 million in 1995. By 1995, overall graduate enrollment was 185, with particular increases in women, minorities, and international students.[5]

What became known as the *Delaware Model* of public affairs education was a product of this success. It developed over two decades and grew from foundations set long before the model was fully described and publicly promoted. The key ingredient was the growth of the research and public service centers and the partnerships they supported.

INFORMING DELAWARE DECISION-MAKING

A consultant to the University of Delaware in the mid-1980s, reviewing the interdisciplinary policy-oriented work carried out by the college's faculty, professionals, and graduate students in collaboration with community members and decision-makers, noted: "No other university undertakes these kinds of activities to such a great degree."[6] A 1987 report for the national land-grant universities association (NASULGC) evaluating public service at land-grant universities cited the college as "a model . . . responsive both to external clients and to internal disciplinary concerns . . . and to the needs of the state within the academic context of the university."[7]

Through the 1980s and 1990s, the centers established during the Division of Urban Affairs's formative years expanded their capacities, enabling the accelerating formation of partnerships. The Census and Data System had emerged as the critical source for Delaware-related data and data analysis. It maintained an active survey research capacity and designed and developed databases drawn from clients' files. It also used an array of information system technologies to offer ready access to data required for decision-making.[8] Personal computers were introduced, while punch cards and the statistical sorter disappeared. In 1986, the Census and Data System installed one of the first local area networks on the University of Delaware campus, enabling data sharing and work with larger datasets. The system continuously supplied up-to-date information on critical areas of Delaware policy, including health, education, transportation, and economic development. In 1988, the Census and Data System changed its name to the Center for Applied Demography and Survey Research (CADSR).

During this same period, the Institute for Public Administration (IPA) emerged as the primary source of technical assistance to local governments and agencies on planning, policy assessment, and improvements in services. IPA initiated legislative training seminars and policy forums, and undertook municipal management training programs. It also carried out policy and program evaluation projects sponsored by state agencies or the Delaware

General Assembly on such issues as senior center formula funding, public employee compensation reform, the economic impact of tourism, and options for health care financing.

Throughout the 1980s, other centers and individual faculty carried out applied research and public service projects. Jeffrey Raffel became the state's chief expert on Delaware's court-ordered metropolitan school desegregation. The Center for Energy and Environmental Policy worked for the Delaware Public Service Commission, analyzing utility demand and energy efficiency. College faculty and professional staff researched such issues as homelessness, historic preservation, metropolitan services in New Castle County, substance abuse reduction, local economic development, and poverty in Wilmington.[9] In virtually all cases, graduate students worked alongside faculty and professionals to carry out these projects. In addition, by the end of the 1980s, over two hundred graduate students from the college had served as interns for city, county, state, federal, and nonprofit agencies.[10]

Communities throughout Delaware depended on the College of Urban Affairs and Public Policy's expertise for guidance in the development of municipal plans, the organization and performance of administrative operations, the effective delivery of municipal programs and services, the planning of new schools, hospitals, and other service institutions, and the evaluation of policies and practices. Concurrently, collaborations with state agencies also grew. The Delaware General Assembly relied on the college to support its operations and provide staff support for task forces and commissions. Most data and analysis used in public decision-making in Delaware were supplied by or in partnership with the college and its centers.

THE WILMINGTON COMMUNITY DEVELOPMENT PARTNERSHIP

On November 3, 1992, James H. Sills, Jr., was elected the first Black mayor of Wilmington. Sills had been the founding director of the Urban Agent Division, established during the early years of the Division of Urban Affairs. At the time of his election, he was an associate professor in the College of Urban Affairs and Public Policy. As a faculty member, he taught courses on urban management, community development, and human services delivery. Sills also had been president of the Christina School District Board (the largest school district in Delaware) and had been a member and president of the Wilmington NAACP. From 1983 until he was elected mayor, he served as a representative to the Delaware General Assembly. In these roles, Sills expanded the college's partnerships with the educational community and the State of Delaware. He was the leading champion for the development and funding of a new program of public service and applied research that served to support students working alongside faculty and professionals on projects focused on state priorities. That program, later called the Public Service

Assistantships (PSA), became a critical component of the college's graduate programs and public service contributions. When Sills was elected mayor, he took a leave of absence from his faculty position to practice what he had been teaching.[11]

In his inaugural address, Sills announced a new partnership between the city and the University of Delaware that university president David Roselle endorsed. The goal of the partnership was for UD to help the city government meet the needs and promote the development of Wilmington neighborhoods. Known as the Wilmington Community Development Partnership, the new initiative would use the expertise of the College of Urban Affairs and Public Policy and other parts of the university to meet this goal. Roselle said this "new relationship formalizes university outreach to the Wilmington community that has existed for some twenty years and builds upon it to extend our research, public service, and graduate education in community development. At the same time that we are providing these services, our faculty and students will be working and learning in a most exciting 'laboratory'—the largest city in the State." Sills added, "The Wilmington Community Development Partnership is an important opportunity to make a difference in the lives of the people of Wilmington."[12]

The partnership was to be led by the college's Urban Agent Division, renamed the Center for Community Development (CCD) in 1993, concurrent with the launch of the new partnership.[13] From the early 1980s up to 1987, the Urban Agent Division had been led by Babette Johns. She was succeeded by Steven Peuquet, who had joined the staff of the center in 1983. In 1991, as a cost-saving measure and to better integrate the Urban Agent Division with other programs in the college, the unit moved its primary offices from Wilmington to the main university campus in Newark. A small suite of offices was maintained on the university's Wilmington Campus. By 1993, the newly named Center for Community Development's contributions included a growing set of programs and services for nonprofit institutions in Wilmington and across the state, such as the Nonprofit Management Certificate Course, which started in 1990, and over subsequent decades would be responsible for training hundreds of nonprofit managers. CCD also provided direct support for a new interdisciplinary graduate specialization in Community Development and Nonprofit Leadership. In 1994, Timothy Barnekov became CCD's director, and Steven Peuquet returned to a staff position to continue his research and public service work on homelessness, housing, and community information systems.[14]

The first efforts of the center on behalf of the new Wilmington partnership focused on providing technical assistance to public, nonprofit, and community organizations. The center assisted with the analysis of community conditions, development of neighborhood plans, and training of community leaders. Barnekov describes the focus of the work as collaborating with community members, often at the neighborhood level, to build their capacity

FIGURE 16. UD President David Roselle and Wilmington Mayor James H. Sills sign the agreement to establish the Wilmington Community Development Partnership, 1994.

to address the challenges they faced. In that vein, Sills anticipated that the new Wilmington Community Development Partnership would help him strengthen the city's planning department to undertake research and analysis to identify what options might best address the city's challenges. He also called upon the university to help him improve city employees' professional knowledge and qualifications.

The most notable work of the Center for Community Development in support of the partnership focused on capacity-building in Wilmington neighborhoods specifically aimed at strengthening support for collaborative community development programs. This work was already underway when the new partnership was established. A tool of federal government policy during the anti-poverty programs of the 1960s, community-based development gradually lost appeal with the increasing emphasis on privatism and free-market solutions in the 1980s. Despite the withdrawal of federal support, community development organizations in Wilmington and other cities continued to focus on alleviating poverty through action-oriented programs. These organizations constructed new houses and rehabilitated old buildings, created new locally owned businesses that offered employment within the community, improved local community services, and attracted investment in local communities.

Accordingly, the Wilmington Area Community Development Project was one of the major initiatives under the partnership. The project focused on four of the most economically and socially distressed neighborhoods in the city. The impetus came from the Speer Trust Commission, a local foundation, and two area churches that sought to determine the most efficient ways of utilizing their resources to aid the poor. Raheemah Jabbar-Bey, a community development specialist in the Center for Community Development who had previously worked with Sills through the Urban Agent Program, led the project. It began with forums conducted in each targeted neighborhood to involve residents directly in the revitalization effort. These and other mobilization efforts led the Speer Trust to create a community organization fund to benefit emerging neighborhood groups. The project was a harbinger of the community development work that the center would continue into the twenty-first century.

In 1994 and 1995, CCD became one of only a handful of university units in the nation to receive both the U.S. Department of Housing and Urban Development's Community Outreach Partnership Center grant and the U.S. Department of Education's Urban Community Service grant. The funding was used to support a Community Development Resource Center and expand a Housing Capacity Building Program. CCD also initiated a training program in community-based development and received grants from the Longwood, Welfare, and Crestlea Foundations to establish *DiamondNet*, an online community network. In 1994, the center inaugurated the Community Development Certificate Course to help improve the leadership of community organizations that address the needs of low-and moderate-income neighborhoods. Over its first three years, over sixty community leaders completed the program.

The center also focused on supporting programs to address the issue of homelessness and increase the supply of affordable housing. These efforts predated the Wilmington Community Development Partnership and were initially supported in the late 1980s by the Gannett Foundation, the Delaware General Assembly, the Salvation Army, and the City of Wilmington. The center carried out the first statewide study of homelessness. It also sponsored the first statewide conference on the topic, which included 130 national and regional housing leaders from the public, private, and nonprofit sectors. Its work on homelessness and housing grew in the 1990s and beyond, with the center assisting in building new institutional capacity, including the Delaware Homeless Planning Council and the Homeless Management Information System.[15]

CCD's focus on housing and homelessness complemented its work in support of neighborhood-based community development. It also aligned with its work with nonprofit institutions, many of which carried out programs and services related to housing and homelessness. Marvin Gilman was a housing expert, homebuilder, and national leader in affordable housing initiatives who worked with the college and CCD for eighteen years. He applauded the center's initiatives in housing because they were "rooted in real-world issues and challenges" and "because they focused on appropriate and practical solutions for the problem of providing affordable sheltering of all American families."[16]

The collaboration between the Wilmington mayor's office and CCD grew through Sills's second term in office. The center's neighborhood and community development work and its housing initiatives remained the staples of its efforts. However, some Wilmington Community Development Partnership objectives, including the initial expectations of enhanced professional development for city employees, were not fulfilled. The partnership did not continue after Sills left office.

THE EXPANDING GLOBAL REACH

By the 1990s, the College of Urban Affairs and Public Policy had developed a series of international associations that reflected the broader networks formed by faculty and staff, as well as the influence of the international students attracted to the college's graduate programs. Students came from China, Ghana, Greece, India, Mexico, Nigeria, South Africa, South Korea, Syria, and Germany.[17]

The growing global reach of the college is reflected in the story of two of the college's graduates who were responsible for long-term and substantive partnerships with universities and policy institutions in South Africa. Sibusiso Vil-Nkomo was forced to flee South Africa in the 1970s because of his resistance to Apartheid. He met Renosi Mokate at Lincoln University, where they both completed undergraduate degrees and taught before marrying

FIGURE 17. Sibusio Vil-Nkomo, Nelson Mandela, and Renosi Mokate.

and joining the graduate program in Urban Affairs and Public Policy. Mokate received her MA in 1983 and PhD in 1986, and Vil-Nkomo received his MA in 1983 and PhD in 1985. They remained in the U.S. until the release of Nelson Mandela. In 1991, he called them home to help establish the new government. Mokate became the chief executive officer of the Independent Electoral Commission, which in April 1994 administered South Africa's first democratic, multiracial election. Vil-Nkomo became the head of the South African Civil Service and later the first Black dean and then rector of the University of Pretoria. Mokate later became South Africa's representative to the World Bank and executive dean of the School of Business Leadership at UNISA (University of South Africa). Vil-Nkomo later became chairman of the board of the Mapungubwe Institute for Strategic Reflection (MISTRA), a national think tank advising President Cyril Ramaposa and other South African leaders on implementing reforms to achieve greater social and economic equality.

The growing enrollment of international students brought changes in the college's degree programs, research activities, and public service efforts. Many faculty became more internationally oriented, incorporating global themes into graduate courses and developing partnership programs with institutions in other parts of the world. Geographic area specialists—often from other colleges—were included on dissertation committees. The college regularly sponsored international speakers and visiting scholars. In addition, it often developed formal ties with universities and agencies in other nations through its centers, and faculty, staff, and students regularly participated in collaborative comparative international research. The growth of the college's international programs was also encouraged by an increasingly global outlook at the university. There was no central office of international programs, though, so between the 1970s and the 1990s, most international associations and programs were developed by individual faculty and specific departments, centers, or colleges.

Global networking by Biden School faculty can be traced to initiatives in prior decades. For instance, starting in 1975, the college's faculty began sponsoring graduate study abroad programs that focused on opportunities for students to learn how other nations were addressing the issues they were studying in their classes. The study abroad programs took advantage of relationships that grew out of the partnerships developed by the college's faculty and professionals. The first program, led by Arno Loessner and Jerome Lewis, enabled graduate students to study planning and intergovernmental relations models in London, Paris, and Amsterdam, leveraging relationships Loessner had cultivated with local government agencies.[18] Shortly after being appointed university secretary and chief of staff to UD's president in 1978, Loessner also initiated a partnership with the Salzburg Seminar, a nonprofit that convenes scholars and practitioners from across the world to address critical global challenges. That partnership provided opportunities for college faculty and staff to participate in week-long workshops with the convened seminar participants. The seminars were held at the program's headquarters in Austria and focused initially on policy issues related to the relationship between the U.S. and European nations, later engaging more global issues.[19]

By the 1990s, study abroad became a feature of the college's graduate programs for which the University of Delaware and the college provided partial scholarships. The college was among the first public affairs programs in the U.S. not only to offer and support international educational opportunities for graduate students, but also to build these opportunities into the design of the curriculum. Starting in the 1990s and expanding later, formal partnership agreements with universities and public agencies in other nations supported study abroad programs in the Netherlands, Scotland, Romania, South Africa, and South Korea. Many faculty and professionals in the college took advantage of these programs, which also led to visiting scholars spending time at UD, extending relationships and partnerships that remained active through the subsequent history of the Biden School. For example, the college had a long-standing relationship with the Centre for Planning at the University of Strathclyde in Scotland. The two institutions hosted faculty exchanges, beginning with a visiting faculty position at the center for Barry Cullingworth. This collaboration also created opportunities for student exchanges. Additionally, teams composed of faculty and staff from both programs co-authored publications.[20] One multi-year collaborative project borne of this relationship focused on comparing urban policy and planning in the US and the UK.[21]

The college's centers were also actively engaged in international programs. IPA created an office of research and training to deal with global issues. In 1996, the University of Delaware, supported by IPA, and the International Union of Local Authorities, the worldwide association of local governments based in The Hague, Netherlands, signed a partnership agreement. Their newly created program became known as the International Union of Local Authorities-Office for Research and Training or IULA-ORT. It offered seminars for local government officials and elected leaders in Mexico, Africa, Eastern Europe, Korea, and Panama.[22] The Center for Applied Demography and Survey Research also became engaged in international programs through the work of Edward Ratledge. He participated in a seven-year comparative study of prosecutorial decision-making across the world's criminal justice systems.

The college's faculty and professionals also were called upon as international consultants: Bernard Herman worked with the U.K. Commission on Historic Monuments, and Robert Warren was an advisor to cities in Japan on the use of telecommunications in urban development. In 1990 alone, the college hosted a dozen visiting scholars from Cameroon, Finland, Korea, Poland, Spain, Sweden, and Syria.

The most extensive and consistent international focus came from the faculty, staff, and students in the Center for Energy and Urban Policy Research, renamed the Center for Energy and Environmental Policy (CEEP) in 1993. The center was one of the nation's earliest academic research and teaching centers to focus on the interrelated areas of energy and environmental policy and to do so through an interdisciplinary and policy-oriented research framework.[23] The center's work concentrated on the political economy of energy and how it could be changed.

In 1990, the center received funding from the World Bank to study alternative institutional approaches to help four Southeast Asian countries (Indonesia, Malaysia, South Korea, and Thailand) pursue economic objectives in environmentally sensitive and energy-efficient ways.[24] The study recommendations influenced the practices of both the World Bank's and the United Nations' development programs and the policies of the four countries. Center Director John Byrne led such global research. He argued that this work was a natural extension of the mandate that led to the College of Urban Affairs and Public Policy's creation and inspired its development for thirty years: "[T]he issues of urbanization, poverty, and inequality are global, and it is essential that our college be able to grapple with them. We need to address the crises of energy, environment, and urban development that are affecting the lives of people all over the world with the same urgency that we sought to address American urban policy issues."[25]

FIGURE 18. John Byrne (PhD, UAPP 1980), professor and director of the Center for Energy and Environmental Policy, 1984–2021.

In 1997, CEEP became an official observer organization to the United Nations Framework Convention on Climate Change, which enabled the submission of briefing papers that became part of the official record; ultimately, CEEP submitted ten briefing papers.[26] CEEP also oversaw an Energy and Environmental Policy Series, publishing books focused on critical global issues in the political economy of environmental and energy policy.[27] This series involved faculty from several disciplines and attracted graduate students who wanted to work on the global issues of climate change, energy transformation, renewable and nonrenewable energy options, environmental justice, and later smart cities and sustainable development.

The faculty engaged in this global research proposed a new interdisciplinary master's and doctoral degree program in Energy and Environmental Policy, known by its acronym ENEP.[28] The ENEP program was approved in 1997, with the first official enrollments in 1998. The first graduates received their Master of Energy and Environmental Policy (MEEP) in 1999, and the

FIGURE 19. Young-Doo Wang (PhD, UAPP 1980), professor, 1983–2014, and director of the Energy and Environmental Policy Program, 1997–2014.

first ENEP PhD graduated in 2001. Young-Doo Wang, associate director of CEEP, became the ENEP program director, a position he held until 2014. The program drew upon faculty from many colleges and, because of its global orientation, attracted most of its students from outside the U.S. Many students were from China, India, South Korea, and other nations where CEEP already had ongoing research partnerships. The graduates from the ENEP program thus became part of a growing network of global research collaborators focused on energy and environmental policy, sustainable development, and climate change.

THE *DELAWARE MODEL*

The growth of the research and public service centers and the partnerships they supported provided the foundation for what became known as the *Delaware Model* of public affairs education. In 1995, Robert Denhardt joined the college as the Charles P. Messick Professor in Public Administration. He soon became an advocate for writing about and promoting the *Delaware Model*, wanting to increase its visibility to the national public administration community. He hoped that writing about the success of this unique model would stimulate a rethinking of the typical structure of public affairs programs.

Denhardt, Jerome Lewis, Jeffrey Raffel, and Dan Rich undertook a series of publications and presentations at professional meetings about this distinctive approach to public affairs education. The *Delaware Model* was most fully examined in a jointly authored article by the four faculty members in the *Journal of Public Administrations Education* in 1997.[29] Recognizing that the dichotomy between theory and practice had "haunted the field of public administration," including public administration education, they proposed that a new educational approach that engaged students in the integration of theory and practice as a fundamental part of their learning experience was needed. Enabling that approach required more than a simple redesign of the curriculum. Instead, programs should be designed in terms of the total experience of students, such as it was at Delaware: "The University of Delaware College of Urban Affairs and Public Policy has developed a model of public administration education that seeks to build upon the student's total experience in such a way that theory and practice are fully integrated." This effort, they pointed out, was not only based on the curriculum but also part of the design and operation of the college itself.[30]

They described the features of the college that enabled the *Delaware Model* to thrive, pointing out that all faculty and professional staff were expected to reflect the integration of theory and practice in their own contributions and engage graduate students to participate with them in the programs and projects that required such integration. As a result, the educational experience was not limited to students' classroom activities but also included daily involvement in researching important policy issues, preparing

training and development programs for those in public agencies, and inter-
acting with officials at all levels of government and in nonprofit organizations
of all types. Students were fully involved in projects—gathering and analyzing
data, organizing conferences, and writing and presenting policy recommendation reports. Typically, the students were funded by assistantships supported by grants and contracts from government or nonprofit institutions. The
article's authors argued that the result was a student body well prepared to
enter responsible positions in public service and make substantial contributions from the outset. In the long run, the integration of theory and practice
that students experienced in their MPA program would make them more
effective learners able to adapt to change throughout their careers.[31]

The *Delaware Model* benefited from the annual funding the university
received from the State of Delaware General Assembly, which supported
graduate students working on public service and applied research projects of
vital interest to Delaware's communities and agencies. The Public Service
Assistantship program (PSA), which began receiving funding in 1985, had its
funding increased in the 1990s, helping to support the expansion of the
college's graduate programs, particularly at the master's level. PSA funding
was often used as match support for small grants from public agencies and
community organizations, enabling partnerships that otherwise would not
have been possible or would have been much smaller. The 1994 PSA budget
allocation, for example, supported graduate student work with college
faculty and professional staff on forty projects. PSAs assisted the Wilmington
Housing Authority, the Governor's Public Utility Regulation Task Force, the
Delaware Community Reinvestment Action Council, the Delaware Superior
Court, the Delaware Division of State Service Centers, and the Delaware
Domestic Violence Council.

Another program that embodied features of the *Delaware Model* was the
Legislative Fellows Program. The program, a partnership between the Institute for Public Administration and the Delaware General Assembly, was
established in 1985 and grew through the 1990s. Graduate students and later
also advanced undergraduates were annually selected through the program
to serve as legislative staff and provide research and operational support to
legislative committees, task forces, and caucuses. The General Assembly
provided funding for the program with supplemental support from the
university. The students selected received a full-tuition scholarship and a
stipend to support living expenses, and enrolled in a course on state government while they worked in the legislature. IPA Director Jerome Lewis
describes the program, which continues as of 2021 as a co-sponsored effort
with Delaware State University, as "a hands-on learning experience for
students" through which they "are able to observe and contribute to the
decision-making process while working with individuals with diverse views
and values such as state and local government officials, business and community leaders, and concerned citizens."[32]

The staff of the Delaware General Assembly is small compared to legislatures in other states and, as a result, Legislative Fellows have played a more central role in legislative activity than typical interns.[33] The program has also led many fellows to pursue careers in public service, particularly in the Delaware state government. The General Assembly has hired some of these students upon their graduation.[34] John Carney (MPA 1986), who became the Seventy-Fourth Governor of Delaware in 2017, has described his time as a Legislative Fellow while completing his MPA degree as a "transformational experience.... It helped me determine that the best way for me to help others and improve the community was through politics and public service."[35]

In 1996, a review committee appointed by the provost concluded that the College of Urban Affairs and Public Policy "has moved into its third stage of development with national ranking as a 'purposeful' college for the 21st Century." The committee report pointed to the *Delaware Model* as a primary reason for the college's success: "The integrated model of education, policy research and public service, using centers as designated areas of specialization has served the college and the state well." The report also proposed that this integrated model "improved the quality of academic programs" and contributed to greater national and international distinction for the college's programs while also strengthening the work of its research and public service centers. The report applauded the "improved quality, visibility, and recognition of college's research and public service programs in the state, the nation, and the international community," and argued that the university should ensure that the "college's unique integrated model of teaching, research, and service and its productivity be expanded."[36]

PART II

BECOMING A
COMPREHENSIVE SCHOOL

(1997–2014)

FIGURE 20. Leland Ware, Louis Redding Chair in Law and Social Policy, with high school students designated as Junior Redding Scholars and UD graduate and undergraduate student mentors, 2001.

CHAPTER FOUR

THE SCHOOL OF URBAN AFFAIRS AND PUBLIC POLICY

EARLY IN THE 1990s, from almost the beginning of his tenure, President David Roselle questioned whether the configuration of the University of Delaware's colleges matched the university's priorities for the future. Most of UD's ten colleges, including the College of Urban Affairs and Public Policy, were small. Some colleges were organized to address needs that were pressing during an earlier period in the university's history, so the mix of programs in some colleges no longer had a compelling logic. Roselle was also concerned with the administrative cost of maintaining numerous small colleges, each with a dean and dean's staff, and with redundant expenses to support services for a modest number of faculty, staff, and students.

Beyond campus considerations, external pressures also influenced the reevaluation of the college configuration. The Business Public Education Council (BPEC), a coalition of business and education leaders, formed in 1990 and openly advocated for greater university involvement with public education. Many Delaware public schools, particularly those in Wilmington, were struggling. Roselle believed that a merger of the College of Urban Affairs and Public Policy with the College of Education would connect the experience in applied research and public service on state policy issues provided by the former with the expertise in best practices in education and teacher preparation cultivated by the latter.

The responsibility for orchestrating the reconfiguration of colleges fell to Provost Melvyn Schiavelli.[1] In September 1995, Schiavelli charged the deans of the colleges likely to be affected with determining if UD was organized in the best way to maximize program strength and achieve the greatest possible intellectual synergy between related programs. In response, the deans concluded that the current organization of colleges was inadequate and in need of change. The option they recommended was a consolidation of five colleges into two new colleges. One consolidation would include the colleges of Education, Human Resources, and Urban Affairs and Public Policy. The other consolidation would include the College of Nursing, the College of Physical Education, Athletics and Recreation, and related health and fitness programs.[2]

The process moved forward swiftly based on the deans' recommendation. On July 1, 1997, the College of Human Resources, Education and Public Policy was launched. Two years later, the name changed to the College of Human Services, Education and Public Policy, known by its acronym CHEP. The former College of Urban Affairs and Public Policy became the School of Urban Affairs and Public Policy, one of six academic units in CHEP.[3] The administrative leadership of the new college came from members of the College of Urban Affairs and Public Policy. Daniel Rich was appointed the first dean and served until he became university provost in August 2001. He was succeeded as dean by Timothy Barnekov, who had served as associate dean of the College of Urban Affairs and Public Policy.[4] Both were inclined to apply features of their former college to CHEP.

FIGURE 21. Timothy K. Barnekov, dean, College of Human Services, Education and Public Policy, 2001–2007.

As the new college was taking shape, Rich described it in terms that echoed the College of Urban Affairs and Public Policy's mission. CHEP would become "an interdisciplinary, professional, service-oriented college that would address some of the central and interrelated intellectual challenges of our times . . . a tangible 21st-century expression of a dynamic, responsive and innovative land-grant institution enriched and extended beyond any other model to date."[5] CHEP's mission and objectives, developed by a faculty and professional staff group during the transition to the new college, focused on creating and applying "knowledge about the interconnected challenges facing children, families, schools, communities, the environment, and public, private and nonprofit organizations."[6] CHEP would also prepare professionals to assume leadership positions in public, private, and nonprofit organizations and promote collaborations that encourage more effective policies and management in all sectors.

While CHEP was being created, the Kellogg Commission on Higher Education, working on behalf of the Association of Public and Land-Grant Universities, advocated a new university model, the *engaged university*. The commission's work was motivated by changes in the global political economy of higher education, including those pertaining to resources, technologies, and public expectations. Through reports over five years in the mid-1990s, the commission proposed that the *engaged university* would address emerging social needs and priorities by creating and using knowledge to better serve the community.[7] As advocated by the commission, the *engaged university* would establish broad societal impact as a benchmark of achievement. It was anticipated that increased public funding would be attracted to support that effort.[8] This was a vision of the land-grant tradition writ large. It defined

BECOMING A COMPREHENSIVE SCHOOL

a campus-wide mission that would mobilize students, faculty, staff, and university leaders to make community engagement a central part of institutional operations and scholarship. The commission stated: "Engagement must become part of the core mission of the university,"[9] echoing the mission of UD's new college.

THE EXPANDED STATE PARTNERSHIP

The College of Human Services, Education and Public Policy was the vehicle for an expanded partnership between the university and the State of Delaware designed to mobilize the new college's applied research and public service capacity to support state priorities. The key to this partnership was CHEP's center-based strategy, an extension of the research and public service model of the College of Urban Affairs and Public Policy that focused on issues regarding public education and services to children, families, and low-income communities.

The creation of CHEP aligned with the priorities of then-Delaware Governor Thomas Carper. He had created the Family Services Cabinet Council to focus on integrating programs and services across state agencies, particularly those addressing education, human and social services, community development, and the needs of children and families, especially those in poverty. The alignment of priorities translated to increased state resources to support the work of the new college. Starting in 1997, and for the next decade, the university annually submitted requests for additional state line-item funding for CHEP programs above the state allocation that supported general operations. Most of those requests were approved.[10] Before the college merger, the programs that became a part of CHEP collectively received less than one million dollars in designated state line support. Most of this funding went to programs in the College of Urban Affairs and Public Policy. By FY2001, recurrent state line funding for CHEP increased to nearly $4.4 million. The increased funding was targeted at specific programs, but the benefits were college-wide. For example, state funding doubled for the Public Service Assistantship program, a crucial component of the *Delaware Model.*

The new partnership between the state and CHEP focused largely on strengthening the university's support for improving Delaware public education and providing direct assistance for educational reform. In addition to enhancing programs for teacher education, UD expanded professional development programs for teachers, educational administrators, and others who served Delaware schools and children. Most of these efforts were undertaken by CHEP, although they involved collaboration with secondary education programs in the College of Arts and Sciences and education-related programs in other colleges.[11] CHEP launched new and expanded programs in early childhood education and development, disabilities studies and special education, parenting, school board training, school finances and management, and education policy evaluation, and increased support services for children and families.

The state partnership also led to the creation of four new CHEP research and public service centers to support the improvement of public education. The Math and Science Education Resource Center (MSERC) and the Delaware Center for Teacher Education (DCTE) were created to strengthen teachers' professional development. The Delaware Education Research and Development program, which had been part of another unit, was established as an independent center within the college to provide information and analysis about the condition and performance of the educational system in the state. The fourth new unit was the Center for Disabilities Studies (CDS), which focused on improving public and private services for individuals with disabilities and their families.[12] Each center received direct state funding to supplement support from the university and from external contracts and grants.

The new state partnership significantly impacted the centers that had been part of the College of Urban Affairs and Public Policy. The Institute for Public Administration became the home of the Delaware Academy of School Leadership, which provided professional development and technical assistance for district and school administrators. IPA's Office of Conflict Resolution assisted in the mediation of disputes in schools and communities. IPA also initiated programs in education management training and school finance and infrastructure planning. IPA's Democracy Project, headed by former Delaware Secretary of State Edward Freel, offered a unique professional development opportunity in civics education for Delaware social science teachers, enabling them to engage with government and community leaders at all levels. The Delaware Social Studies Education Project, which sponsors in-service professional development for teachers, was initiated by a partnership between the IPA and DCTE.

Other centers added programs complementary to the new partnership. The Center for Community Development was renamed the Center for Community Development and Family Policy to engage the faculty and students in CHEP's Department of Individual and Family Studies. It became the home of the Delaware Kids Count program, supported by the Annie E. Casey Foundation, which tracks the health and well-being of Delaware's children. The center also launched a Nonprofit Capacity Building Program to strengthen the contributions of Delaware's nonprofit sector to the overall improvement of communities throughout the state. The Center for Applied Demography and Survey Research developed a new database for school finance information, conducted regular statewide surveys that covered education and human service issues, and provided demographic data supporting enrollment projections for Delaware school districts. CHEP became the primary research, planning, technical assistance, and professional development arm for Delaware's public education and human service agencies. The college forged new education partnerships in all parts of the state.[13]

CHEP also served as the administrative home for other state and community program initiatives. Public Allies Delaware (an AmeriCorps program) joined the Center for Community Development and Family Policy, and DCTE sponsored the Delaware Mentoring Council. CHEP centers regularly convened public policy forums and conferences to address key Delaware policy issues, especially in education and social services. The college also issued policy reports and evaluations of state practices. Many of the programs launched through CHEP's partnership with the state continued for the next two decades, especially those focused on improving Delaware public education and services for children and families.

SUAPP

By the late 1990s, all of the leading comprehensive public affairs programs across the U.S. were professional schools. The former College of Urban Affairs and Public Policy faculty wanted the University of Delaware program to have the same designation. Thus, when the College of Human Services, Education and Public Policy was created, the School of Urban Affairs and Public Policy (SUAPP) became the first new school approved by the university since the trustees' decision in 1964 to convert all previous schools to colleges.

Jeffrey Raffel became the founding director of the newly designated school and served in this capacity for the next decade. Raffel had joined the Division of Urban Affairs in 1971 after completing his PhD at MIT. Before serving as SUAPP director, he had been the director of the MPA program. From the outset of his appointment, Raffel focused on strengthening the school's reputation. Some of his efforts focused on marketing the school's programs, which had not been done earlier in any methodical way. The school developed a new newsletter, the first school website, and a branding of the *Delaware Model* under the slogan "Make a Real Difference," which became the

FIGURE 22. Jeffrey A. Raffel, director, School of Urban Affairs and Public Policy, 1997–2007.

centerpiece of the school's graduate recruitment efforts. However, the larger objective was to gain greater national recognition for SUAPP among peers in the public affairs education community. The school systematically pursued that objective during Raffel's tenure, and, over the next decade, its reputation as one of the nation's leading comprehensive public affairs programs grew.

The orientation of CHEP was aligned with the school's priorities, and the school benefited from the addition of resources to support the new college.

Raffel discovered, however, that not all facets of the new college helped the school. When CHEP was created, the centers and institutes from the merging colleges remained at the college level. The rationale was that they were the bridges between the university and the communities it served. This arrangement created a challenge for the school. The academic programs and faculty appointments were in the school itself and under the administrative responsibility of the school director. However, the centers that generated funding to support SUAPP's academic programs and the *Delaware Model* were operating college-wide, and their directors reported to the dean.[14] The school director held the same responsibilities as a department chair and, as Raffel recognized early on, lacked the authority over the centers the earlier leaders of the program held when it had college status. In his reflections on that period, Raffel declares that his most difficult day-to-day challenge was the school's dependence on centers that were not under his authority.[15]

This split structure led to cumbersome ongoing negotiations between the SUAPP director and the center directors.[16] Even so, the funding support provided by the centers for graduate students in the school increased continuously over the new college's first five years, a product of the increased funding of the centers from the state and the growth of external grants and contracts. In addition, a university policy adopted in 2003 provided a matching tuition scholarship for students on a graduate research contract who received their stipends from an external grant or contract, so long as overhead charges were applied to the stipends.[17] This doubled the dollars provided for graduate student support. Raffel recalls that this "was the Golden Age of the school's student financial aid almost certainly unequaled in public affairs graduate programs in the nation."[18] By September 2005, the school had over one hundred graduate research assistants and fellowships, most funded from external grants and contracts.[19] Under the new arrangement, the *Delaware Model* was flourishing.

DRIVING DIVERSITY

Building on the original mandate of the Division of Urban Affairs, enhanced during its years as an independent college, the School of Urban Affairs and Public Policy was a university leader in promoting racial and ethnic diversity. The early foundations for this role were established with the initial staffing of the Division of Urban Affairs and notably the Urban Agent Program led by James Sills. By the early 1990s, the College of Urban Affairs and Public Policy's graduate program had been recognized for its leadership in minority enrollment and retention. In 1993, the MPA received a special citation from the university's Commission to Promote Racial and Cultural Diversity for its success in "the recruitment and retention of African-American graduate students and for, consistently over the years, leading the university in the percentage of graduate students who are African-American."[20] The previous year, the provost's review committee had confirmed that "the MPA program consistently attracts more Black Americans and Hispanic students than any other graduate program."[21] The committee added that "the college's three graduate programs collectively account for about 20% of all minority graduate students at the university."[22]

One of the primary reasons for SUAPP's success in minority recruitment, retention, and graduation was the consistent personal effort put forth by faculty, staff, students, and administrators. James Sills and Betty McCummings, who led the MPA program in the early 1990s, were both graduates of historically Black colleges and interested in urging undergraduates from those colleges to attend the University of Delaware for graduate study. Beyond recruitment, there was a consistent focus on student development, a feature of the *Delaware Model*. Many graduate classes focused on policy topics related to the intersecting challenges of poverty, race, community development, and social justice. In addition, the graduate programs were notable for gender diversity. When the school was created, most of its graduate students were women.

In 2000, as the result of a successful development effort, the university established the endowed Louis L. Redding Chair in Law and Social Policy in the school. Redding was Delaware's premier Black civil rights leader and the lead attorney on the case that resulted in the desegregation of the University of Delaware. He was also the lead attorney on two Delaware cases that became part of the Supreme Court's *Brown v. Board of Education* decision declaring segregation in public education unconstitutional. Leland Ware was hired as the first Redding Chair, with the explicit mandate to strengthen SUAPP's research and instruction on civil rights issues and racial and ethnic equality. Ware, a Boston College Law School graduate, had worked with the U.S. Department of Justice and was on the Saint Louis University Law School faculty. His scholarship focused on civil rights and segregation. One of Ware's first initiatives was the Redding Young Scholars, a year-long academic enrichment program that paired high school students with UD undergraduate and graduate student mentors to prepare participants for leadership roles in law and public service. Ware's appointment, Raffel recalls, "reinforced the school's engagement in Wilmington and the minority community and brought a senior legal scholar to the school. Ware also helped with the recruitment of minority students."[23]

Ware became an outspoken advocate for the school's leadership role in increasing diversity at the university. He later reflected on that role: "[The school] has long been a leader in promoting diversity on UD's campus and in the surrounding communities. The composition of [the school's] faculty and student body make it the most diverse academic unit on UD's campus. Our students and faculty work closely with several community organizations that serve African American and Hispanic constituencies."[24] In 2001, SUAPP's strategic priorities affirmed its commitment to diversity as a shared value and a core dimension of quality. In that same year, the UD Commission to

Promote Racial and Cultural Diversity selected the school to receive the Louis L. Redding Diversity Award for its effectiveness in recruiting and supporting diverse students and faculty and for addressing issues of racial and cultural equity in its instruction, research, and public service programs.

PUBLIC SERVICE FACULTY AND PROFESSIONALS

Most senior professionals affiliated with the School of Urban Affairs and Public Policy contributed to its instructional programs and engaged in research and public service through the College of Human Services, Education and Public Policy's centers; many had secondary faculty appointments. In 2001, those senior professionals carrying out faculty responsibilities were converted to non-tenure track public service faculty, and became members of the faculty collective bargaining unit, the American Association of University Professors (AAUP). The conversion worked well for the school since it formally recognized the critical role of the senior professionals in the success of its academic programs. The problem, however, was that the funding for their positions often depended on defined responsibilities for applied research and public service rather than for academic instruction or longer-term scholarly research. Barnekov recalls that the non-tenure track public service faculty often sought extensive involvement in teaching, advisement, and thesis and dissertation supervision in the academic programs.[25] Many of the professional staff in the school who were not converted to non-tenure track faculty also had solid backgrounds in research, and many were interested in teaching. As the graduate programs grew, more were called upon to teach master's level classes and supervise students, including many students who worked on externally funded projects.

For some professional staff, these circumstances created a conflict between their applied research and public service assignments and their desire to teach, supervise students, and publish in academic journals. In 2002, Barnekov, with the provost's support, proposed that at least 10 percent of the workload for professionals with secondary faculty appointments be designated for scholarly research. While implementing this proposal was an official acknowledgement of the issue, the action was largely symbolic. In practice, this modest allocation did little to alleviate the conflict in roles and responsibilities SUAPP's senior professionals were facing.

CHEP's practice of placing new tenure track faculty on extended appointments to its centers posed a different but related challenge. In addition to their traditional nine-month academic year contract, these faculty received two months of summer support to participate in externally funded research and public service. The expectation was that the extended appointments would eventually be self-supporting since the new faculty would become more active in developing external grants and contracts.[26] However, the difficulty in engaging faculty in the centers' applied research and public service programs became more acute as UD developed a stronger identity as a research university. Faculty success measures increasingly emphasized refereed publications and scholarly citations over projects focused on improving communities or policies. While some new faculty worked across teaching, scholarly research, and public service domains, most made limited contributions to public service and applied research. The idea of an integrated orientation toward scholarship that connected teaching, research, *and* public service was not consistent with the university's incentive structure for faculty promotion and tenure.

THE NEW UNDERGRADUATE MISSION

Proposals for the school to develop a role in undergraduate education long predated the creation of CHEP. For example, the 1992 university-level review of the then-College of Urban Affairs and Public Policy had called for its faculty to play a role in undergraduate education by teaching some courses and offering applied learning opportunities to undergraduate students. Still, the review affirmed that the college should not offer a major or minor and should remain a graduate unit. Now that the School of Urban Affairs and Public Policy was part of the second-largest undergraduate college at UD, the university leadership's expectations were quite different. The occasion to support an undergraduate program came from a reorganization within CHEP.

When the College of Human Services, Education and Public Policy was formed, it included the Department of Consumer Studies, a unit of the previous College of Human Resources. The department focused on undergraduate education and had two separate program areas: Consumer Economics, and Apparel Design and Fashion Merchandising. Each area had dedicated faculty and degree programs, and the two programs were developed along quite different pathways. Recognizing that the new college offered opportunities for program reorientation and redesign, and with a growing faculty scholarly interest in the field of leadership, the Consumer Economics faculty in 2001 redesigned their major to become Leadership and Consumer Economics. They also added a minor in Leadership. In 2004, at essentially the same time as the department reorganized, the major's name was changed to Leadership. The provost and the CHEP dean then proposed that the Leadership program and its faculty should join SUAPP, as the undergraduate program was developing in ways aligned with graduate programs in the school that focused on public and nonprofit leadership.

To Raffel, the proposed move seemed like an excellent opportunity for the school. He recounts, "In short, this was a way to get seven new faculty or faculty lines instantly, have a successful undergraduate program," and get the administration "off our backs" for not playing a sufficient role in undergraduate education.[27] Despite these advantages, some of SUAPP's faculty considered adding the undergraduate program to be incompatible with the school's focus on graduate education. Ultimately, despite some dissent, the move of the Leadership program was approved by the faculties of both units. The head of the program, Karen Stein (PhD, UAPP 1984), argued that students majoring in Leadership would have expanded opportunities through the school. These benefits would include "more prospects for conducting under-graduate research because of the ready access to a larger faculty, the availability of more internships, and SUAPP's numerous partnerships with governmental and nonprofit agencies."[28]

The addition of the Leadership undergraduate program launched a new phase in the school's development. Within ten years, SUAPP would have over five hundred undergraduate students pursuing three different academic majors and four minors. The school also would become a leader in combined programs that enabled highly qualified students to complete a bachelor's degree and then a master's degree in five years.

EXEMPLIFYING THE ENGAGED UNIVERSITY

Reflecting on the School of Urban Affairs and Public Policy's development after his second five-year term, Raffel recalls being pleased by what had been accomplished. He was particularly proud of the improvement of student recruitment, the addition of an undergraduate program, and the growth of the graduate programs. "We were graduating over 60 graduate students annually."[29] Beyond its specific accomplishments, SUAPP was becoming better recognized as one of the nation's premier comprehensive public affairs schools. Raffel had set this as a priority at the outset of his tenure as director. While some of the school's faculty continued to be active in urban affairs, Raffel and others participated more in the national public administration associations, the American Society for Public Administration (ASPA) and the National Association of Schools of Public Affairs and Administration (NASPAA).[30] The latter was significant since it was the accrediting association for public affairs programs, having a tremendous impact on the reputation and recognition of those programs, and included the directors of all of the major public affairs programs across the nation. Raffel joined its accreditation commission for master's programs and chaired it from 2003 to 2005. He later served as chair of the accreditation standards revision committee and became NASPAA vice president in 2008 and president in 2009.[31] Other SUAPP faculty became regular contributors to NASPAA and ASPA programs and remained engaged with the Urban Affairs Association.

Robert Denhardt had been instrumental in building the school's reputation in the 1990s by making the *Delaware Model* better known and appreciated within the national public affairs field. He left the school in 2000 and vacated the endowed Charles P. Messick Chair in Public Administration. The same year that Raffel was appointed founding director of SUAPP, he was also appointed the new Messick Chair, a position he held until his retirement, after which it was awarded to his successor as director of the school, Maria Aristigueta. A provision of the original Messick endowment was that a portion

FIGURE 23. Maria Aristigueta appointed Charles P. Messick
Chair of Public Administration in 2013, with previous holders of that chair,
William W. Boyer (left), Robert Denhardt, and Jeffrey A. Raffel.

of it would support a distinguished visiting scholar each year, designated the Messick Fellow, who would come to campus for a short period to deliver lectures and work with faculty and students. Those subsequently appointed Messick Fellows became part of a growing network of distinguished affiliated scholars that further enhanced recognition of the school.

By 2002, *U.S. News & World Report* ranked SUAPP among the top fifty public affairs schools in the nation. The school retained its high ranking as seventh in the nation in urban policy and city government. The school also gained recognition in nonprofit management, which led to a national ranking in that specialization in subsequent years. The School of Urban Affairs and Public Policy's reputation as a nationally ranked, comprehensive school of public affairs was indisputable.

By 2006, in many ways, UD exemplified the model of the *engaged university*. In that year, Rich addressed the national meeting of the Consortium of

University Public Service Organizations hosted at the university. He titled his presentation: "The University of Delaware as an Engaged University." He argued that UD was among the most public universities. This was not because of state funding but because of UD's impact across the First State. UD was a land-grant, sea-grant, space-grant, and urban-grant institution, and the only comprehensive research university in a small state. It was called upon to fulfill responsibilities that would have been met in larger states by government agencies, quasi-governmental institutions, or many different universities.[32] UD was an indispensable partner of state and local government agencies and of nonprofit institutions in providing expertise and technical assistance to improve the quality of life in communities across Delaware. In particular, Rich pointed to the contri-

FIGURE 24. Daniel Rich, provost, 2001–2009.

butions of SUAPP and CHEP as exemplifying the model of a twenty-first-century engaged university.[33]

On May 23, 2006, David Roselle announced that he would step down as UD president at the end of the next academic year, marking seventeen years of service. Roselle had been the architect of the modern University of Delaware. Under his leadership, UD was transformed from a good-quality regional institution into one of the nation's finest public universities. For the Delaware community, the most critical transformation was that the university was now serving more Delawareans with a broader array of programs than ever before, and both the School of Urban Affairs and Public Policy and the College of Human Services, Education and Public Policy were instrumental in that change.[34] Roselle's tenure had strengthened UD's role as an engaged university.

CHAPTER FIVE

THE SCHOOL OF PUBLIC POLICY AND ADMINISTRATION

ON JULY 1, 2007, Patrick Harker became the twenty-sixth president of the University of Delaware. Harker had been a highly successful dean of the Wharton School at the University of Pennsylvania, expanding its programs and resources.[1] He was known as an innovator with documented success in fundraising, promoting new university-business partnerships, and raising Wharton's global visibility and recognition. Harker was recruited with a mandate from the leadership of the Board of Trustees to pursue the same goals at UD, with the focal point being accelerating growth in research and graduate education.

When Harker arrived, UD was already an anchor institution in the Delaware economy. The university was one of the top ten employers in the state, that ranking only increasing in the early 2000s as other state employers such as DuPont and MBNA contracted.[2] UD was also a hub for advanced research in emerging technologies, such as biotechnology, solar cells, and composite materials. Between 1990 and 2005, its annual federal research and development funding more than doubled, rising from $40 million to $85 million.[3] This growth in federal funding was expected to accelerate under Harker's leadership. The former dean of the world's premier business school would be the architect of UD as an entrepreneurial research university, as David Roselle had been the architect of UD as an engaged public university. That general mandate translated into a specific benchmark for success: earning membership in the American Association of Universities (AAU), representing America's leading research universities.[4]

Harker's push to become a premier graduate and research university was part of a larger strategic plan named the Path to Prominence that would advance the overall development of UD. The plan was designed to inspire high aspirations, and it was well balanced across the university's core areas of undergraduate education, graduate and professional education, and advanced research. However, there was a significant difference between such balanced objectives and the priorities reflected in the new budgeting system developed to fund university operations. Responsibility-Based Budgeting (RBB) was introduced to incentivize federally funded research. For example, larger amounts of undergraduate tuition revenue would be allocated to units generating high levels of funding from federal contracts and grants.[5] State funds also were allocated based on an algorithm that rewarded units generating federal funding rather than those carrying out research and public service for the state.

Without a medical school or law school, increasing UD's profile as a research institution and attracting private investment to support that goal focused on strengthening the College of Engineering, the Lerner College of Business and Economics, and interdisciplinary science and technology programs such as the Delaware Biotechnology Institute. Harker launched new initiatives such as the Delaware Health Sciences Alliance, the UD Energy Institute (UDEI), and the Delaware Environmental Institute (DENIN) to bundle the university's research capacity across academic units and external partners.[6] These collaborative initiatives offered opportunities to attract sizeable federal research and development grants and contracts.

RECESSION AND RECOVERY

The implementation of the University of Delaware Path to Prominence was abruptly interrupted by the Great Recession of 2008, the impact of which was immediate and dramatic. UD's endowment plummeted, and its state appropriation dropped by $15 million. Federal research dollars were cut, and expectations of launching a major private fundraising campaign evaporated. More families struggled to pay students' expenses, which placed additional demands on the university's financial aid resources. In response to these conditions, the university implemented budget cuts in administrative and non-academic units, deferred hiring, and postponed facility improvements.

Beyond the immediate impacts, the period after the onset of the recession changed the underlying economics of higher education at most universities, including UD. The Center on Budget and Policy Priorities reported that state governments spent, on average, 28 percent less per student on higher education in 2013 than they did in 2008.[7] For the University of Delaware, by 2012, state support had declined to about 12 percent of its total budget. Meanwhile, the level of federal research and development funding through the years of the economic recession remained relatively flat compared to pre-recession levels.[8] However, many universities, including UD, competed more intensely for a relatively fixed amount of federal support. UD's federal research funding continued to rise through 2010 but then sharply declined.[9]

At the same time, the costs of delivering higher education continued to rise at a rate that outpaced traditional sources of revenue. These higher costs were driven by increased expenses for facilities, technology, administration, and employee salaries and benefits. As the economic downturn slashed university endowments, fewer options were available for filling the growing gap between costs and revenue. In response, public colleges and universities increased tuition charges, and some issued debt to finance long-term goals.

At UD, tuition rates had been rising even before the recession. Between 2000 and 2015, in-state tuition increased by 84 percent (from $6,805 to $12,520, adjusted for inflation to 2015 dollars). However, during that same period, median household income in Delaware dropped by roughly 14 percent.[10] A few years after the onset of the recession, Harker affirmed to the UD community that difficult decisions would have to be made. However, the university had to remain focused on its priorities. "We need to focus on creative programs, research activities, and partnerships that will drive the university forward," Harker stated. As UD's financial resources contracted, however, the vision projected by the Path to Prominence narrowed, with public affairs education and public service losing their place in that vision.

This reflected the challenges that public affairs programs across the nation were experiencing in the wake of the recession. In 2010, Francis Berry became president of the Network of Schools of Public Policy, Affairs, and Administration (NASPAA). In her presidential address, she proposed "that our programs—perhaps more than ever—have to demonstrate our purpose for existing; and our relevance to students, our universities, and our broader communities."[11] Berry concluded that public affairs programs and the public service values they embody were no longer valued as they had been for the previous half-century. During that time, the dominant vision had been that universities would apply their expertise to address America's critical social and economic issues at all levels, from those affecting neighborhoods to those affecting the nation, from the War on Poverty to the Cold War. As the vision of the public purpose of universities had constricted, the regard for public affairs programs eroded. The financial crisis of 2008 and subsequent economic downturn accelerated the decrease of public funding for higher education, leading university officials to justify budget cuts to programs that exemplified more expansive public responsibilities. The squeeze on program funding often was accompanied, Berry noted, by a shift in the prevailing models of university budgeting.[12] Under the new models, academic units were treated as cost centers that had to be justified either by providing compensating revenue or through becoming an institutional priority.

"Delaware First" was one of the guiding principles of UD's Path to Prominence strategic plan. However, the interpretation of that principle became narrower, particularly after the onset of the recession. The university administration requested that state line items, many of which directly supported programs and services of priority to the state, be rolled into UD's overall state operating budget allocation. The legislature declined these requests but did agree to bundle the state lines as allocations to the colleges rather than to specific programs, leaving it to the deans of the colleges to determine how the state funds would be used. Reduced in-state tuition rates for graduate students were eliminated, which was particularly problematic for a graduate-oriented school like the School of Urban Affairs and Public Policy. University funding for public service programs and public service staff was cut, and no new faculty with primary public service responsibilities were to be appointed.[13]

CHEP UNDONE

From the time he arrived at the University of Delaware, President Harker questioned the rationale for the College of Human Services, Education and Public Policy. He viewed it as a forced marriage of units that had distinct missions and that should have a different configuration within the overall architecture of the university. Harker was familiar with freestanding professional schools of education and did not see the value of combining education with public policy. Instead, he thought that public policy was best pursued in connection with substantive areas of inquiry and he had little interest in a comprehensive school of public affairs.

CHEP faced problems even before Harker arrived. From the outset, some faculty in the School of Education believed their school should remain a separate academic unit. Further, the projected added value from bringing the smaller colleges together under the shared CHEP banner had not materialized. While these academic units operated under the same college, there was little collaboration. Earlier plans for shared facilities that would bring faculty in these units into physical proximity to one another were never implemented.[14] While the CHEP centers worked collaboratively, none of the anticipated academic collaborations between the School of Education and the School of Urban Affairs and Public Policy succeeded.[15]

Once the start-up phase for the new college ended, each unit prepared a strategic plan that reflected its expectations and aspirations. Not surprisingly, most of these priorities were program-specific and did not focus on the integrated development of CHEP. Jeffrey Raffel has acknowledged that the School of Urban Affairs and Public Policy focused on a desire to strengthen its own identity rather than that of the college. This focus was inevitable, Raffel claims: "Who identifies with their college rather than their program? What faculty member indicates what college they are in instead of their department or school, i.e., the closest unit to them and/or their discipline?"[16] For the most part, CHEP remained an amalgam of academic units rather than an integrated whole.

During Harker's tenure, CHEP would come under direct challenge as a result of two events. In August 2007, Barnekov announced his retirement as dean of CHEP effective at the end of the next academic year, and a national search was launched for his successor. However, the search failed when the search committee did not recommend a candidate. Harker saw the failed search as further evidence that CHEP was an obstacle to raising the prominence of UD's education programs. After the search failed, Michael Gamel-McCormick, director of the Center for Disabilities Studies and former chair of the Department of Human Development and Family Studies, was appointed interim dean in July 2008 and named dean in May 2009. To raise the profile of the education programs in CHEP, he proposed a change in the college's name to the College of Education and Public Policy. This action was approved but did little to mollify those interested in a complete reconfiguration of programs.

The second event was Rich's announcement to the University Faculty Senate on March 9, 2009, that he was resigning as provost effective June 30. Thomas Apple, dean of the College of Arts and Sciences (CAS), was named the incoming provost.[17] He confirmed his intention to replace the College of Education and Public Policy with a comprehensive College of Education that would absorb the secondary education programs in CAS that enrolled about half of UD's teacher education students. Apple's proposal generated almost immediate resistance from the CAS secondary education faculty, who believed that their students should continue to be educated in the academic disciplines that they would be teaching. Even so, Apple proceeded with his plan.

On March 17, 2010, Apple announced Gamel-McCormick's resignation as dean of CHEP, at which time he also announced several changes under consideration for the college, including moving the School of Urban Affairs and Public Policy to the College of Arts and Sciences. He proposed that moving the school under CAS would have many benefits. It would strengthen the social sciences, enhance SUAPP collaborations with other programs (such as the new Center for Political Communication), and provide additional educational and research opportunities for the school's students. He later acknowledged that some faculty wanted the school to form its own college, as it had been until the late 1990s, but this option, he believed, would not be viable given the RBB budget system.[18]

In May 2010, the UD Board of Trustees approved creating the College of Education and Human Development, which would no longer include the School of Urban Affairs and Public Policy. No decision had been made about the school's future. As an interim measure, it would report directly to the provost as a freestanding unit until a permanent resolution was presented to the Faculty Senate in the next academic year. The controversy continued into the fall of 2010. At that point, the school's faculty concluded that becoming an independent college or professional school would not be supported by the university administration, so they voted to join the College of Arts and Sciences.

Maria Aristigueta, who succeeded Jeffrey Raffel as SUAPP director in 2007, had been on the faculty for a decade and had a strong record of academic leadership.[19] It was left to her to navigate the school's development through the period of CHEP's dissolution. One of her first steps was to establish a steering committee to plan for the transition. The steering committee recommended that the centers that had historically been affiliated with the

School of Urban Affairs and Public Policy should move with it and become units within it. The compelling logic, supported by the center directors, was that the school and its centers would be stronger together.[20] The exception was the Center for Energy and Environmental Policy (CEEP) and the Energy and Environmental Policy (ENEP) program, which would move to the College of Engineering to strengthen faculty collaboration in technology and policy.[21]

The faculty and staff also voted to change the school's name to the School of Public Policy and Administration to reflect the broader scope of its programs. In November 2010, the University Faculty Senate approved a resolution to implement a move of the entire school to the College of Arts and Sciences with the new name School of Public Policy and Administration (SPPA), effective July 1, 2011. Despite these organizational changes and negative shifts in the university's outlook on public service programs, the school maintained a strong base of support among state leaders, some of whom were alumni and many of whom remained committed partners. That became evident when the school celebrated its fiftieth anniversary.

THE FIFTIETH ANNIVERSARY

On March 19, 2012, less than a year after the School of Public Policy and Administration joined the College of Arts and Sciences, more than three hundred alumni, friends, and partners, as well as faculty, staff, and students assembled at a reception at Clayton Hall to celebrate the school's fiftieth anniversary. University administrators, members of the state's congressional delegation, and other state leaders applauded the school's impressive legacy and commended its vision for the future. President Harker joined the celebration. "When we talk about UD's service mission—when we talk about a 'Citizen University'—we're talking about the School of Public Policy and Administration," said Harker. "It's at the heart of service scholarship—research applied to public policy and the public good."[22] U.S. Senator Thomas Carper, who had actively supported the school during his tenure as Delaware's governor, praised the expertise and commitment to public service demonstrated by the faculty, professional staff, and students. He said that they helped him and other decision-makers "address the critical issues facing our state and nation and, in a practical manner, helped all levels of government."[23]

While the school was applauded as the heart of the university's service scholarship, it was located in a college with other priorities. The growing challenge for the school as an academic unit was to adapt to the culture and policies of the College of Arts and Sciences, which meant becoming more like a traditional social science unit. Even so, after being in limbo for nearly two years, there was a distinct benefit in being part of UD's largest college. Aristigueta points out that CAS provided a safe haven under the new and somewhat unpredictable RBB funding system. However, the college had very little

FIGURE 25. Director Maria Aristigueta and UD President Patrick Harker
at the Biden School 50th Anniversary Celebration, March 19, 2012.

FIGURE 26. U.S. Senator Thomas R. Carper (left) and former Delaware Secretary of State Edward Freel, speak at the 50th Anniversary Celebration, March 19, 2012.

knowledge and experience with overseeing professional programs, interdisciplinary policy-oriented research, or centers designed specifically for applied research and public service.

Aristigueta appointed Leland Ware as associate director of the school to focus on adjustments it needed to make as part of CAS. From the time of his initial appointment at the university, Ware had collaborated with CAS faculty and contributed to some of the college's programs. He was familiar with many CAS policies and took the lead in crafting some of the changes to SPPA policies that were needed to align the school with the college, including those on faculty promotion and tenure criteria and procedures. Ware also served as interim director for the 2012–13 academic year while Aristigueta was on sabbatical leave.[24]

When it joined CAS, the school, predominantly a graduate unit, became aligned with other social science units mainly serving undergraduates. In its first few years in the college, SPPA faculty teaching loads were changed. Only traditional nine-month academic year faculty appointments were approved, and restrictions were placed on hiring public service faculty and professional staff. Some of these changes reflected the tightening of the university budget because of the recession. Other changes were designed to bring the school in line with CAS policies.

FIGURE 27. Leland Ware, associate director (2010–18) and interim director (2012–13, 2014–15), School of Public Policy and Administration.

George Watson, who became dean of CAS when Apple was appointed provost, took deliberate steps to enable SPPA's smooth transition to the college. Even though state line items were now under the control of the college, Watson reserved the funding for the programs for which the line items were originally allocated. In addition, Watson agreed that the school could establish a board of advisors. Given the challenges of the previous few years, Aristigueta and some senior faculty believed that SPPA needed an organized group of advocates to protect its interests and promote its development.

Chaired by G. Arno Loessner, then an emeritus professor, the SPPA Board of Advisors held its first meeting on March 19, 2012. The board's mission was to support sustained communication between the school's leadership and leaders in the broader community. Its objective was to mobilize increased support for SPPA's programs and development. Accordingly, its members included alumni and donors, as well as leaders of the diverse constituencies the school served.[25] Some members, such as John H. Taylor, Jr., executive director of the Delaware Public Policy Institute, a unit of the State Chamber of Commerce, represented the school's partners.[26] Others were prominent

FIGURE 28. School Board of Advisors members Daniel Rich (left), John H. Taylor Jr. (executive director of the Delaware Public Policy Institute), Arno Loessner (chair of the Advisory Board), and Leland Ware at the March 19, 2012, School Career Conference.

state and federal policy leaders, such as Jeffrey W. Bullock, Delaware's Secretary of State, and Jane Vincent (MPA 1995), U.S. Housing and Urban Development regional administrator for the mid-Atlantic.

THE EXPANDING UNDERGRADUATE
AND GRADUATE MISSIONS

Despite the challenges of the transition and reductions in university funding from 2008 to 2014, the School of Public Policy and Administration was able to add academic programs. The new programs aligned with UD's emerging budgetary priorities and took advantage of SPPA's location within CAS. One of the most critical priorities was to enhance the school's undergraduate mission.

The school had first offered an undergraduate program in 2005, with the transfer of the Leadership program to its purview. Even so, the school's culture remained unmistakably focused on graduate education. That began to change with the move to CAS. A major and minor in Public Policy were established in 2010 and approved for permanent status by the university in spring 2014. Initially directed by Audrey Noble and later by Dan Rich and Andrea Pierce, this program provides undergraduates with access to many experiential learning opportunities previously available only to graduate students.[27] A minor in Public Health was also established in 2010 in collaboration with the College of Health Sciences. The undergraduate Leadership major was renamed Organizational and Community Leadership (OCL). Along with the name change, the curriculum was revised to focus on helping students understand the complexities of leadership in solving organizational and community problems.

Like the graduate programs, all SPPA undergraduate programs were distinctively interdisciplinary. They also promoted active, discovery-based learning that offered pathways to promising professional careers. The school's undergraduate programs attracted students who wanted to prepare themselves to make a difference in the organizations and communities in which they would work and live. These programs grew dramatically after 2009. In the fall of that year, SPPA had 161 undergraduate majors and minors, all in Organizational and Community Leadership. At that time, the school had slightly more graduate students than undergraduates. Four years later, it had 542 undergraduate students across the OCL, Public Policy, and Public Health programs.[28] By 2014, the number of SPPA undergraduates was three times the number of graduate students.[29] Notably, overall College of Arts and Sciences enrollments, including those in the other social sciences, were flat or declining during this same period.

This growth in undergraduate education was significant not only for the students who now benefited from learning opportunities previously unavailable to them, but also for the faculty. In 2009, most of the school's faculty continued to teach at the graduate level, with only a small fraction teaching regularly at the undergraduate level, but by 2013, most of them were engaged in both undergraduate and graduate instruction. The transformation in faculty workload was often challenging, as was the change in the predominant, exclusively graduate culture. However, school faculty agreed that, in the future, they would all regularly teach both undergraduate and graduate students.

The school was now making available to undergraduates the character and quality of educational experiences that graduate students had benefited from for decades. SPPA undergraduates were encouraged to participate in service learning and undergraduate research, often working side-by-side with faculty and graduate students on projects that helped translate ideas into policy and program initiatives for communities and organizations. These experiences also prepared students for success after they graduated. SPPA undergraduates were now eligible to become paid Summer Public Policy Fellows, working on research and public service in one of the school's centers. They were also eligible to become Legislative Fellows, an opportunity earlier available only to graduate students.

Another such opportunity arose in 2012, when Ed Freel of the Institute for Public Administration initiated a Washington Fellows Winter Session program that enabled twenty undergraduates to spend a month in Washington, DC, taking courses on policy and politics taught by UD faculty and participating in internships with public and nonprofit organizations. The program, led by Freel himself, subsequently became a full-semester option offered in collaboration with the Colin Powell School of Civic and Global Leadership at the City College of New York.[30] The faculty of both institutions taught courses including frequent guest lectures by public and nonprofit leaders and opportunities for students to serve as interns with congressional committees, executive agencies, and advocacy organizations.

By 2014, excellence and innovation in undergraduate education had become part of the institutional signature of the School of Public Policy and Administration. Rather than conflicting with other facets of SPPA's mission, this growing dimension of its identity dovetailed with and enhanced those other facets. One of the best examples of this was the establishment of three 4+1 options for highly qualified Public Policy majors in 2010. These options enable students to complete both a BA in Public Policy and one of three SPPA master's degrees in five years. Even in the first years of the 4+1 options, it became clear that they supported the educational aspirations of exceptionally motivated and capable undergraduates. Some of them became outstanding students in the school's graduate programs, which continued to thrive and expand. For instance, the Disaster Science and Management (DISA) MS and PhD degrees were initiated in 2010, and the program moved administratively to SPPA in 2011.[31] Sue McNeil, a professor of Civil and Environmental Engineering with a joint faculty appointment in the school, became the first director of the program, which took advantage of the university-wide interdisciplinary faculty capacity in disaster science and management.

FIGURE 29. Joe Biden visiting University of Delaware Washington Fellows, winter 2015.

FIGURE 30A James Kendra and **FIGURE 30B** Tricia Wachtendorf,
co-directors, Disaster Research Center.

The backbone of the program was the work of the Disaster Research Center (DRC), which was established in 1963. The center was the first in the world devoted to the social scientific study of disasters. Social scientific research was still one of DRC's core products, even as the center expanded into interdisciplinary work. Historically, center faculty and students had conducted field interviews and extended research projects on community preparation for, response to, and recovery from natural and technological disasters. All DRC research was intended to yield both basic scientific knowledge and information that could be used to develop more effective plans and policies to reduce the impacts of future disasters. Because of this, DRC attracted funding from diverse federal agencies.[32] While not a formal part of SPPA, the center had a close collaborative relationship with the school. DRC codirectors James Kendra and Tricia Wachtendorf had faculty appointments in SPPA, as did other core DRC faculty. The center was also physically located adjacent to the school. The DISA graduate program was developed to take advantage of the DRC's strengths and recognition, so when the program was created, it was natural that SPPA would be its home.

MEETING THE MARKET CHALLENGE

When the School of Public Policy and Administration entered the College of Arts and Sciences, it was the largest social science graduate unit in the college and among the largest at the university. The MA and PhD degrees in Urban Affairs and Public Policy were among the nation's oldest, most well-regarded urban policy-focused programs. Consistent with this standing, in 2012, SPPA was ranked twelfth in City Management and Urban Policy by *U.S. News & World Report*. In 2011, the National Research Council had ranked SPPA's PhD in Urban Affairs and Public Policy twelfth among all doctoral programs in public affairs, public policy, and public administration. NASPAA had fully and continuously accredited the MPA since 1982. In 2012, its accreditation was renewed for another six years.[33]

Despite this success, the school's graduate enrollment became difficult to sustain. The MPA program experienced a significant decline; full-time enrollment fell from sixty students in 2009 to thirty in 2013, and part-time enrollment dropped from nineteen to ten over the same period.[34] Some of that decline was undoubtedly a product of the impact of the recession. It became difficult for individuals to afford full-time enrollment, especially as employers reduced or eliminated reimbursements for education. However, other factors were much more consequential than the changing national and regional economy.

The MPA enrollment decline was largely the result of changes in university policy. Delawareans faced a doubling of tuition costs because the university had significantly increased graduate tuition while eliminating in-state graduate tuition rates. Many Delawareans selected programs at other institutions or simply did not pursue an advanced degree. By 2009–10, the

UD MPA program was among the most expensive in the nation, and the cost was rising. A 2013 analysis of revenue impacts of graduate tuition policies submitted by the SPPA to the CAS dean documented that its MPA program was more expensive than other highly ranked MPA programs in the U.S., including those ranked higher than UD's. Further, most universities offered discounted rates to at least some students, and many provided tuition discounts to most students. Competing programs at most public universities continued to provide in-state tuition rates. Even many private universities offered significant discounts on the sticker price of their MPA programs.[35]

The conclusion from the analysis was clear: "The University of Delaware MPA program has been priced so that it is no longer competitive in the regional, national or global marketplace."[36] As a result of this analysis, Aristigueta negotiated with CAS Dean Watson for a scholarship program that effectively reduced the cost of tuition for in-state applicants and those working in the public and nonprofit sectors. However, the sticker price for the MPA program remained higher than that of the SPPA's national competitors, and the actual cost was higher than that of many regional competitors. Even with the newly approved scholarships, fewer paying students enrolled since most had easy access to lower-priced options.[37] The result was declining enrollment and lower net revenue for the university and the College of Arts and Sciences.[38]

THE CRITICAL CHALLENGE

Despite its many accomplishments, in addition to grappling with declining graduate enrollments, the School of Public Policy and Administration faced a severe challenge after moving to the College of Arts and Sciences due to the loss of faculty. Between 2009 and 2014, the number of SPPA faculty declined from thirty-two to twenty-six. Most of the loss was due to the retirements of faculty hired during the 1970s and 1980s. Two more faculty retirements brought the faculty down to twenty-four in 2015, a reduction of 25 percent since the late 2000s. The retirements included faculty who played central roles in the graduate and undergraduate programs. With limited resources to meet the needs of its many academic units in the wake of the recession, CAS did not approve the replacement of the faculty who left. In addition to the faculty reduction already experienced, the school expected further retirements over the next five years.

Including cuts in state funding, the total loss to the school in recurrent funding was over $2.23 million from 2009 to 2014. To address these losses, SPPA streamlined its graduate programs, redesigned its undergraduate programs, filled some faculty vacancies with temporary appointments and supplemental (adjunct) faculty, and made up for some of the lost university revenue through increased external contracts and grants. However, the situation was not sustainable and could not continue without a decline in program quality.

The reduction of faculty numbers translated into more than a loss in overall university financial support. The decrease in faculty numbers had profound implications for the delivery of academic programs, most immediately the school's graduate programs. Between 2011 and 2014, most SPPA academic programs were redesigned because of this diminishing faculty capacity. In some cases, the redesign was dramatic, as it was for the PhD in Urban Affairs and Public Policy. The faculty responsible for more than 75 percent of the dissertation supervision over the previous twenty years were no longer with SPPA and were not replaced. The MA in Urban Affairs and Public Policy and the MPA programs were revised to allow the sharing of some core courses between them and to reduce the number of specialty courses required for each degree. The MPA was streamlined to thirty-six credits (from forty-two), making it a more viable and competitive option for paying students, particularly part-time and 4+1 students. These changes helped in the short term, but they did not compensate for the loss of faculty resources.

BIDEN PROPOSALS

When SPPA entered the College of Arts and Sciences, Maria Aristigueta reported to Joseph Pika, associate dean for the social sciences, who had been an advocate for the school, helped facilitate its transition to CAS, and recognized and supported its need to operate differently from other CAS units.[39] Pika also was one of the first individuals to advocate for greater university recognition of alumnus Joe Biden by placing his name on important programs and initiatives. Pika's colleague Ralph Begleiter, a former CNN correspondent and Rosenberg Professor of Communication, was the most active advocate for the university to name an important initiative for Biden. More than a decade before SPPA joined CAS, Begleiter and Pika recognized that opportunity. Begleiter argued, "To a non-Delawarean familiar with the national and global reputation of Delaware's senior Senator, it seemed inconceivable in 1999 that the state's flagship university had no Biden library, Biden statue, Biden lecture hall or Biden program of any kind honoring its famous alumnus."[40] Pika recalls that "we talked about the issue on several occasions and agreed that Biden could be an asset, particularly on international issues because he was then serving as chair of the Senate Foreign Relations Committee."[41]

In 2003, Begleiter had submitted a memo to Vice Provost for Academic Affairs Bobby Gempesaw proposing the establishment of a Biden Center for Strategic and International Studies. The Biden Center would be "a major galvanizing initiative toward internationalizing the university campus and would significantly raise the visibility of the University of Delaware on both the national and international scenes."[42] The university administration did not pursue the proposal. At about the same time, Susan Brynteson, Vice Provost and May Morris University Librarian, was discussing with the provost the prospect of the university housing Biden's senatorial papers and what would be required to effectively store and preserve the papers, and make them available as a scholarly resource. Biden did not indicate that he was leaving the Senate at the time, and no consideration would be given to the donation of his papers until he was at the end of his senatorial career.[43]

The university administration became enthusiastic for proposals to recognize Biden once he was confirmed as Barack Obama's running mate at the Democratic National Convention in the summer of 2008.[44] President Harker expressed interest in developing such proposals and had several conversations with Begleiter and others to encourage the fleshing out of ideas.[45] Pika and Begleiter stepped up their advocacy for the university to support a Biden-linked initiative to strengthen international studies and the social sciences. Those efforts were further encouraged by the increasing media attention on the university. In 2008, Bloomberg News characterized the University of Delaware as the "epicenter of politics" because Biden, President Obama's campaign manager David Plouffe, John McCain's chief strategist Steve Schmidt, and newly elected New Jersey Governor Chris Christie were all UD alumni.[46] On CBS News, *New York Times* columnist Frank Bruni called UD a "maker of political kings."[47] Begleiter reports that "amid this unexpected national profile, the concept of a Biden Institute was developed very fully, with much consultation among faculty, administrators, and other campus leaders."[48] In 2010, the Center for Political Communication (CPC), headed by Begleiter, was created as a step toward a larger plan.[49]

An important part of Pika and Begleiter's proposal was a new building that would house the social sciences and a new Biden Institute (previously referenced as the Biden Center).[50] Pika recalls that they made the building "a centerpiece of the forward-looking conversations" and referred to it as the "Interdisciplinary Institute for Politics and Policy" since, under a formal agreement signed at Biden's request, there could be no use of his name associated with any university project until he "retired from any public office."[51] As conceived, the institute would be a core facility that would house social science units and have the capacity to support campus and community engagement with political leaders and policy-makers on critical issues to the nation and the world. The prospective site for its building was just south of the Morris Library in the last remaining space in the original campus plan for the Green. Pika publicly announced the prospect of the institute during one of UD's Alumni Weekend events, and there was some preliminary planning for how such a building might most effectively be utilized.[52] However, while President Harker expressed strong and continued interest in the institute, he prioritized other building projects.[53] While a fundraising plan was developed, it was not implemented, partly because of limitations on using Biden's name while he was serving as vice president. Pika and Begleiter attempted to work around these limitations, collaborating closely with CAS and university development staff.[54] Despite these efforts, Pika concludes, "we could not find a way to pry out the funding necessary for getting the project off the ground."[55]

The donation of Biden's senatorial papers, however, was moving ahead. On September 16, 2011, Vice President Biden came to campus to sign the agreement to have his senatorial papers housed at the University of Delaware, as well as to deliver the James R. Soles Lecture on the Constitution and Citizenship. Biden focused his presentation on the importance of the Constitution as a framework for civil discourse, enabling many different voices to be heard and providing the institutions through which they may be blended. He urged UD students to get involved in public service: "Politics is not a dirty word. Politics is the only way a community can govern itself and resolve its differences without the sword."[56]

President Harker thanked Biden "for this extraordinary donation of Senatorial papers, an abundance of materials that will illuminate decades of U.S. policy and diplomacy and the vice president's critical role in its development." The papers, Harker said, would provide students and scholars "an incredible asset for generations to come."[57] Begleiter also thanked Biden for donating his senatorial papers. He said the university expected someday to have "an institute built around the policy themes to which Joe Biden has devoted his lifetime of public service—constitutional law and equal justice, political participation and responsible citizenship, economic opportunity and prosperity, effective government, and foreign policy and international relations."[58] In June 2012, Biden's senatorial papers were delivered to the University of Delaware Library. A separate section of the library was set aside to store, process, and preserve the materials, which consisted of 1,875 boxes.[59]

In 2014, David Wilson succeeded Pika as associate dean for the social sciences.[60] For Wilson and CAS Dean George Watson, the School of Public Policy and Administration's location in the college was an opportunity for strategic thinking about interdisciplinary synergy across the social sciences. In 2014, Wilson established a college-wide committee for strategic planning in the social sciences to identify priority areas for scholarship cutting across departments. He proposed that the connective links were in cross-disciplinary strategic values, such as social justice, public service, cultural understanding, well-being, and practices such as analysis, rather in than standard social inquiry topics. For his part, by 2013, Watson had identified a new interdisciplinary social science building as his top priority capital project. At his state of the college address, he proposed that the building be sited next to the University of Delaware Library and claimed that generating funds for this building would be "a major focus" of the college's development effort. Watson said that the new building "will help facilitate . . . cross-disciplinary collaborations," but there was an expectation that the building would specifically house programs and offices for Biden when he completed his second term as vice president.[61]

Wilson led the development of a proposal for a Biden Institute for Social Justice and Civic Engagement, which would be housed in the new building and focus on carrying on the work of Vice President Biden after he left office. Materials, both printed and digital, were prepared to showcase the projected makeup of the building, including future office space for the vice president, public event spaces, and research, exhibition, and public spaces.[62] All of this planning took place in an environment in which the College of Arts and Sciences faced budget deficits that limited its ability to invest in the proposed new social science facility.[63] At the same time, a commitment had been made to build the Interdisciplinary Science and Engineering Laboratory (ISE Lab). That commitment required major multi-year funding contributions from CAS and the College of Engineering, as well as central university funding. No equivalent college and university commitments were made for the social science building.

CHAPTER SIX

SHAPING PUBLIC POLICY

THE CENTERS "are the engines that help drive the school's success and enable it to more effectively integrate education, research, and public service."[1] That was the conclusion of a 2014 external program review of the School of Public Policy and Administration.[2] The external review team's report declared that public service, the scholarship of engagement, was "the very essence of SPPA's identity." Because of that identity, SPPA was an important component of the University of Delaware's mission and priorities and a "remarkable asset to the State and its people."[3]

Through the first two decades of the twenty-first century, the school's centers significantly influenced public policy and the delivery of government and nonprofit programs and services. This influence continued despite declining university funding for public service and reductions in some direct state line-item support. To compensate for these lost resources, the centers and institutes generated more external contracts and grants.[4] Funding from external contracts and grants remained relatively stable between FY 2009 and FY 2014 at nearly $4 million annually, then increased steadily for the remainder of the decade, reaching $6.7 million by FY 2020.[5] The number of research and public service professionals on the school's staff also increased from thirty-three in 2014 to forty-eight in 2020,[6] and the centers and institutes continued to provide significant levels of graduate student support.[7]

The established recognition of these centers as community resources and the experience and skill of their leaders enabled them to navigate the changing fiscal environment. The three programs established in the 1960s and 1970s by the Division of Urban Affairs—the Institute for Public Administration, the Center for Applied Demography and Survey Research, and the Center for Community Research and Service (CCRS)—remained central components of the school. Jerome Lewis had served as the head of IPA since its inception in 1973, and Ed Ratledge had been director of CADSR since 1974. Lewis and Ratledge had statewide recognition, with established networks of government leaders and agencies that regularly relied on their expertise. Other center leaders also held lengthy tenures. Steven Peuquet had been with the Urban Agent Division that became CCRS since 1983, became director of the center in 2005, and served in this capacity until his retirement in 2018. David Ames

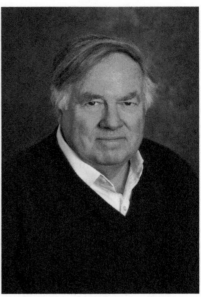

FIGURE 31A Jerome Lewis, Director, Institute for Public Administration,
1973–2021, and **FIGURE 31B** Edward Ratledge, Director,
Center for Applied Demography and Survey Research, 1974–2021.

FIGURE 32. Steven Peuquet, Director,
Center for Community Research and Service, 2005–2018.

served as director of the Center for Historic Architecture and Design from its inception in 1983 until he retired in 2015. John Byrne was director of the Center for Energy and Environmental Policy, a position which he held since 1983.[8]

Another key to the resilience of the centers was the professionals who staffed them. They were mainly funded from external sources, including contracts, grants, and direct state allocations. They assumed more responsibilities as fewer faculty had defined workload assignments in the centers and institutes. The contributions of the centers were also strengthened through better coordination and collaboration. The school hired Nicole Quinn (MPA 2007) as Senior Business Administrator in 2012. She began to develop more collaborative practices across SPPA and its centers, taking advantage of shared resources in processing grants and contracts, managing publications and website development, and other administrative functions. When state and local government resources shrank in the years after the Great Recession, national and state agencies, local governments, and nonprofits could not fill the staff positions needed to carry out required services. They contracted out for services and often turned to those with whom they had worked in the past, such as the SPPA centers.

BUILDING CAPACITY

In 2012, a report prepared for the dean of the College of Arts and Sciences documented the school's public service and community engagement activities for the previous twelve months. It described nearly a hundred separate externally sponsored projects carried out across the state, region, and, in some cases, far beyond.[9] While the specific number and size of projects varied each year, the overall pattern was one of growth throughout the rest of the decade. Beyond the benefits of the particular projects, the contributions of the school's centers fulfilled a vital part of the original mandate of the Division of Urban Affairs: building government and community capacity to make better-informed decisions on policies and services.

The Center for Applied Demography and Survey Research has become the central source for demographic data and projections for state institutions. The Delaware Department of Education and school districts have relied on the center to project changing school enrollments and health care providers have depended on it to advise on the location and effectiveness of services and facilities. State agencies and local governments look to CADSR to inform decisions about fiscal and tax policies, economic and employment options, and transportation system performance. The center also has worked in the Delaware justice system to analyze the processing of cases and study the system's performance. In addition to providing direct services, CADSR has also been an incubator for statewide programs, such as the Delaware Population Consortium, which coordinates demographic information and analysis, and has served as a resource for the Delaware Economic and Financial Advisory Council, authorized by law to project state revenue levels.

FIGURE 33. Elizabeth (Tizzy) Lockman (MA 2015), former Public Ally (2005), teaching at the Biden School after taking office in January 2019 as a Delaware state senator.

Since its creation, CADSR's programs have generated and analyzed data from multiple sources. The center has been a clearinghouse for large data sets supplied by local state, regional, and federal agencies. The center has maintained an active survey research capacity, with the ability to focus surveys on key policy priorities. It also has developed and applied an array of information system technologies, including through the early adoption and use of geographic information system (GIS) tools. These capacities have established CADSR as an essential data resource for the state.

Capacity building for nonprofits and community organizations has been a primary focus of the Center for Community Research and Service. The Nonprofit Leadership Training Certificate Program offered by the center since 1990 has provided professional development for nonprofit staff and leaders. By 2020, the program had more than five hundred graduates, and Delaware nonprofits frequently used the program to prepare younger staff for more senior positions.[10] CCRS has worked to build the capacity of neighborhood and community organizations in Wilmington, an effort that began with the original Urban Agent Division in the 1970s. In 2007, with sponsorship from the Federal Home Loan Bank of Pittsburgh, the Jessie Ball du Pont Fund, and the Delaware Community Investment Corporation, CCRS led the Blueprint Communities program, which engaged residents from selected neighborhoods in making and implementing revitalization plans.[11] The Blueprint Communities program expanded in 2011 and grew over the next decade to include nine Delaware communities, modeling best practices for locally guided development.

CCRS has served as the host for two community-focused programs that celebrated twenty-five-year anniversaries in 2020. Public Allies Delaware (PAD), an AmeriCorps program co-founded by Biden School alumnus Tony Allen (Phd, UAPP 2001), provides leadership training and internship experiences to prepare young adults for public and nonprofit sector positions. The program assigns its allies to work for a year with partner organizations, most of which are nonprofit institutions, while participating in a leadership training program. In 1995, PAD joined CCRS and became one of the few Public Allies programs in the nation hosted by a university. In 2015, PAD received the Impact Award from the national Public Allies organization. As of 2021, more than 650 Public Allies Delaware graduates have contributed over 1.1 million service hours to over 250 nonprofit and government agencies.[12] Delaware State Senator Elizabeth (Tizzy) Lockman, who graduated from the PAD class of 2005 and later earned an MA in Urban Affairs and Public Policy from the School for Public Policy and Administration in 2015, sums up the program's impact: "Public Allies was a turning point for me. My experience as an Ally was eye-opening, giving substance to what I already believed that everyone had value, that we are stronger when we figure out how to work in concert, and that we each have the capacity for leadership. Leadership became a habit, then a lifestyle. I truly believe it does this for every Ally who embraces the program's values!"[13]

CCRS also hosts Kids Count, a program supported by the Annie E. Casey Foundation, which has provided data and reports on the needs of and conditions affecting Delaware's children and families for twenty-five years. The products of Kids Count are frequently cited by advocacy groups and government officials and often serve as the foundation for specific policy proposals, particularly related to education and social services reforms. The location of Kids Count in CCRS also offers easy access to the data on children and families from other units of SPPA, most notably CADSR.

In 2004, an informal health services policy research group led by SPPA faculty members Robert Wilson and Paul Solano and professional staff member Mary Joan McDuffie (MA, UAPP 1988) merged into CCRS. The group focused on evaluating the availability of affordable community-based health care and how to improve that care, applying expertise and experience in health economics, public finance, cost-benefit analysis, and evaluation studies.[14] In 2016, CCRS's role in health policy and analysis greatly expanded. A partnership with the Delaware Department of Health and Social Services supported research to help improve the health of low-income Delawareans and address issues of cost and quality in the healthcare system. Under the agreement, the center became the federally recognized locus for Medicaid research and analysis for the State of Delaware. Stephen Groff, director of Delaware's Medicaid program, wrote that the research carried out under the agreement "enhances our capacity to monitor changes in the Medicaid system, evaluate the effectiveness of various program innovations on the quality and cost of the Medicaid program, and implement effective strategies to improve the overall health of Medicaid beneficiaries."[15] The partnership has also provided opportunities for doctoral students to access data for their dissertations and has supported research that connects health care with other areas of community need.[16] Stephen Metraux, who joined the school's faculty and succeeded Steve Peuquet as director of CCRS in 2018, has used the Medicaid database to document the relationship between housing and healthcare needs. He has also extended the center's research on homelessness, including studies that evaluated the impact of evictions on both the health and needs of vulnerable populations.

FIGURE 34. Stephen Metraux, director, Center for Community Research and Service, 2018.

The Center for Applied Demography and Survey Research has also contributed significantly to healthcare policy. It has conducted behavioral health analyses for the U.S. Centers for Disease Control for decades and has provided demographic data for Delaware's health information system since 2007. The center has also analyzed health and transportation data for health agencies, hospitals, and health professionals, and conducted assessments of the supply and distribution of health professionals, including doctors, nurses, and dentists.

Capacity building in historic preservation planning and practice has been a focal point for the Center for Historic Architecture and Design (CHAD), renamed from the Center for Historic Architecture and Engineering in 1997. CHAD has focused on the documentation and analysis of historic resources, the use of computer applications in preservation documentation, and the use of material culture research and scholarship to provide a context for the interpretation of historic properties. In an important sense, the SPPA's move to the College of Arts and Sciences greatly benefited CHAD. It fits well with college programs and faculty in such areas as Art History and Art Conservation.[17]

CHAD has worked locally and globally. Its collaboration with the Delaware Department of Transportation on the Delaware Byways Program has focused on identifying, promoting, and preserving Delaware roadways that tell important stories about the state's history and scenic qualities.[18] Meanwhile, CHAD has also worked on preserving cultural artifacts in China, building on the work of Chandra Reedy on the preservation of traditional technologies and materials and their cultural heritage in Asia. The center launched one project with Chinese preservation scholars in Sichuan Province to document historic Tibetan buildings, and another with scholars of the Palace Museum to examine the artifacts of the Forbidden City, Beijing.

When the Center for Energy and Environmental Policy rejoined the School of Public Policy and Administration, it was heavily engaged in supporting a new model to promote solar energy adoption, the Sustainable Energy Utility (SEU). The SEU developed directly from CEEP research identifying financing as a critical obstacle to fostering energy efficiency and adopting renewable energy options. Conceived by the center's director John Byrne, the SEU involved a novel financing approach adopted first in Delaware. Kenneth Becker (MA, UAPP 1976) collaborated with Byrne in developing the financial structure supporting the SEU. He describes the SEU as a "one-stop shop." It provides incentives to use less energy and creates revenue sources to pay for the incentives. It encourages cleaner, more efficient energy options and educates the public about the global effects of carbon-based energy usage.[19]

Implementing the SEU model has been a significant step in building capacity for green energy investment. The SEU received White House recognition in December 2011 as part of the country's Better Buildings Challenge, was recommended by the Asia Development Bank to its members for affordable green energy development, and was recognized for its innovation in green energy investment by the International Energy Agency.[20] The SEU model was adopted by other states and cities across the United States and by other nations. The Solar City Seoul, Korea initiative, for example,

FIGURE 35. CHAD faculty Chandra Reedy, Rebecca Sheppard, and David Ames with Chinese preservation scholars (on the left), conducting fieldwork at Jia Jiang in Sichuan Province, China, March 27, 2011.

FIGURE 36. John Byrne, director, Center for Energy and Environmental Policy, addressing the Seoul Mayors Forum on Climate Change, 2019.

resulted in a $500 million municipal financing program for solar and energy savings projects. CEEP director Byrne served on the international advisory council for the project.

INSTITUTE FOR PUBLIC ADMINISTRATION

The Institute for Public Administration has been the largest of the School of Public Policy and Administration's centers and institutes in terms of programs, staff, and student support. By the time SPPA joined the College of Arts and Sciences, IPA had twenty-three affiliated faculty and full-time professional staff. The institute has provided state and local governments with a wide range of services and research findings in land-use planning, local government training and technical assistance, public leadership development, telecommunications, transportation, and public infrastructure. Of particular significance has been its long-term partnership with the Delaware General Assembly, which includes the Legislative Fellows program and ongoing contracts for staff support and technical assistance in assessing policy and service options. IPA developed a comparable partnership with Delaware's local governments through its long-term collaboration with the Delaware League of Local Governments. For more than three decades, this collaboration has resulted in the creation of programs serving municipalities of all sizes across the state. These programs range from certifying municipal clerks to informing local officials about emerging issues in local planning, land use, technology (such as community broadband access), and service-delivery models.[21] Another alliance with the Delaware Public Policy Institute, a think tank sponsored by the State Chamber of Commerce, led to the development of an ongoing series of public forums on key policy challenges such as improving public education, enhancing economic development, increasing energy choices, and maintaining environmental quality. The forums often highlighted key University of Delaware initiatives in each of these areas, including the launch of new partnerships and new university units to address critical policy issues.[22]

FIGURE 37. Kathleen M. Murphy, associate director, IPA, 2015–21; coordinator, Conflict Resolution Program, 2000–21.

IPA has housed and supported units that might otherwise have been independent centers. For example, IPA's Conflict Resolution Program, led by Kathleen Murphy, focused initially on the mediation of disputes in schools as an alternative to court proceedings and provided mediation training to teachers and other educators.[23] The program expanded to provide nonprofit organizations and local and state governments with meeting facilitation, strategic planning, and team-building services.

FIGURE 38. U.S. Senator Thomas R. Carper discusses water resource policies with the staff of the Water Resource Center, 2016.

One of IPA's most important long-term contributions has been in water resource planning and management, leading it to house Delaware's Water Resource Agency and later the federally designated Water Resource Center. Since 1977, the institute has worked with an alliance of local and county governments on water resource issues in New Castle County. That role grew in 1998 when Delaware's Water Resource Agency (WRA), which evolved from the alliance, became a part of IPA. WRA engaged in research and technical assistance to enhance the quality of water resources throughout Delaware and the surrounding region, which provides 10 percent of the water supply for the U.S. In 2016, WRA's responsibilities expanded when it merged with the Water Resources Center (WRC), designated as part of UD's land-grant responsibilities. The recently merged WRC has received federal and state funds to provide ongoing research and technical assistance to local and state governments.

Gerald Kaufman, the director of WRC since 2016 and previously director of WRA, has held faculty appointments in the Biden School, the Department of Civil and Environmental Engineering, and the Department of Geography. He pursues a distinctively regional approach to water management and policy since the watersheds and aquifers that provide drinking water to Delaware cross many political jurisdictions. Most water resource policies and practices in Delaware and the surrounding region reflect the influence of WRC and WRA research and technical assistance. Kaufman calls Delaware the "First State in Water," proposing that the conservation of its water resources is a product of decades of bipartisan policy collaborations at the state and regional levels, all of which have actively engaged the expertise of WRC and WRA.[24]

IMPROVING EQUITY IN DELAWARE PUBLIC EDUCATION

The School of Public Policy and Administration influenced Delaware public policy in many domains, but in none more consistently and consequentially in the second decade of the twenty-first century than the promotion of educational equity.[25] Since the 1990s, the Institute for Public Administration has made significant contributions to improving public education by providing professional development programs for school and district leaders, civics education for social sciences teachers, analysis to aid in improving school finances and facilities, and technical assistance to support the Delaware Department of Education's efforts to increase college application rates.

IPA's work on educational equity began in 2009 with significant contributions to early childhood education policy in Delaware, particularly focused on supporting the Delaware Early Childhood Council (DECC), appointed by the governor and mandated by state law to recommend improvements in early childhood policies, programs, and practices.[26] Dan Rich became chair of the DECC in 2009, and IPA systematically supported the council's initiatives, with leadership being provided by the institute's Ed Freel and Kelly Sherretz. Sherretz (MPA 2004) coordinated all of IPA's education programs.

A comprehensive inventory sponsored by DECC identified nearly one hundred different state policies affecting early childhood services. Some were at cross-purposes and administered and financed by different state agencies with little coordination. DECC had earlier developed a quality rating improvement system, Delaware Stars for Early Success (Stars), based on national best practices for delivering early childhood services. However, there was no incentive for providers of those services to participate in Stars.[27] In 2010, the council proposed the implementation of such incentives along with an increase in the state's funding of early childhood program expenses for low-income families. Despite cuts in many areas of the proposed 2011 state budget, Governor Jack Markell recommended and the Delaware General Assembly approved an investment of $22 million in new recurrent funding for high-quality early childhood initiatives aligned with the Stars standards. This funding was the largest new ongoing spending priority in the state, providing low-income families access to higher-quality programs.

FIGURE 39. Kelly Sherretz (MPA 2004), Policy Scientist and Educational Services Coordinator, Institute for Public Administration.

Researchers from IPA and CADSR provided ongoing analysis of early childhood service issues and options for DECC. With funding obtained from a federal planning grant, Sherretz led a statewide needs assessment to determine the availability of quality early childhood services, prepared policy briefs on state policy choices regarding early childhood services, and helped develop the DECC website as a resource for parents, providers, and advocates.[28] With federal and state funding, CADSR's Tibor Toth conducted a 2012 study of the Delaware early childhood services workforce that highlighted education levels, benefits provided, and professional development. All of these projects engaged a range of Toth's colleagues in IPA and CADSR, as well as graduate and undergraduate researchers.

As a product of these efforts, in 2012, Delaware was a recipient of a $50 million federal Early Learning Challenge Grant to accelerate the improvement of its early childhood services system, building on the designs developed within the state and incorporating national best practices into all facets of these services. With the additional state and federal funding, the participation of providers in the Stars program grew significantly. The technical support for improvements in service delivery was provided by the state-funded Institute for Excellence in Early Childhood, located at and operated by the University of Delaware's Department of Human Development and Family Services.[29]

In 2013, the State of Delaware officially adopted a new strategic plan for early childhood services developed by DECC with ongoing support from IPA.[30] Kelly Sherretz led the drafting of the document. The plan proposed a comprehensive public/private system that addressed the needs of all children from birth to third grade, with a particular focus on the needs of children from low-income families. On April 15, 2013, U.S. Secretary of Education Arne Duncan traveled to Wilmington to visit early childhood programs and speak about the plan. The plan was presented by Governor Markell and became the framework for policy and practice for the next five years. Some facets of the plan continued to guide policy after the change in gubernatorial administrations. John Carney, who succeeded Markell as Delaware governor, maintained the priority of improving early childhood policy and funding. In 2020, he approved the consolidation of state early childhood programs under the Department of Education, a key recommendation of the Delaware Early Childhood Council since 2013.

In 2014, IPA undertook another major responsibility to support educational equity in Delaware public education, backing the work of the Wilmington Education Advisory Committee, which Governor Markell charged with recommending policies to improve Wilmington public education. In 2015, that group's recommendations led to legislation creating the Wilmington Education Improvement Commission. The legislation designated IPA to provide operational and technical support for the commission. The key priorities of the commission were to streamline the governance of Wilmington public education, provide targeted funds to schools with high concentrations of low-income students and other students at risk, and support programs that offered both in-school and out-of-school services.

The commission's chair was Biden School alumnus Tony Allen.[31] Another alumnus, Elizabeth "Tizzy" Lockman, served as vice chair. The IPA support team included Dan Rich, who served as policy director, and Kelly Sherretz, as well as graduate and undergraduate students.[32] The team produced reports on the state of public education for City of Wilmington students, researched education equity issues, including evaluations of the relationship between poverty and education, and created an inventory of community assets to support Wilmington schools.[33] Most of the commission's educational equity proposals after 2015 cited the research and analysis conducted by IPA, as did plaintiffs in court cases who sought to enhance public education funding for low-income students, English learners, and other students at risk.[34] The resolution of these court cases in 2020 achieved two of the recommendations of the Wilmington Education Advisory Committee. In one case, the court ordered the Delaware counties to undertake property reassessments needed to achieve greater equity in the local tax share of education funding, and the other case resulted in a settlement with the State of Delaware that included $60 million in recurrent state funding for schools with low-income students, English learners, and other students at risk.

FIGURE 40. U.S. Secretary of Education Arne Duncan (left), U.S. Senator Christopher Coons, and Daniel Rich, chair, Delaware Early Childhood Council, at the presentation of Delaware's strategic plan in Wilmington on April 15, 2013.

FIGURE 41. Tony Allen (PhD, UAPP 2001), chair, Wilmington Education Improvement Commission, 2015–19), became president of Delaware State University in 2020.

IPA's work on education equity continued through its support for the Redding Consortium for Educational Equity, created by the State of Delaware in 2019 and mandated to address issues in Wilmington and New Castle County. Lockman, recently elected a state senator, was appointed co-chair. In collaboration with the School of Graduate Studies at Delaware State University, IPA was designated as the support unit for the consortium's work.[35] Haley Qaissaunee (MPA 2017) and Kelly Sherretz coordinated the support work for the consortium even during the COVID-19 crisis. In June 2021, the Delaware General Assembly allocated $10 million in the FY2022 state budget to support the consortium's proposals for enhancing educational equity.

POLICY IMPACTS OF A COMPREHENSIVE SCHOOL

The School of Public Policy and Administration centers' contributions were evident when the school underwent an Academic Program Review in 2014. The self-study portion of the review affirmed SPPA's emergence as a comprehensive school.

Today, SPPA is a globally recognized, comprehensive school of public affairs. SPPA has six graduate degree programs, two undergraduate majors, three undergraduate minors, four research and public service centers, and another affiliated research center. SPPA engages in sponsored and unsponsored research and policy analysis, and provides technical assistance to a wide range of governmental, nonprofit, and community institutions. SPPA's reach and influence are greater now than ever. The ongoing accomplishments of our faculty, professionals, and students have been amplified by an extensive range of partnerships with institutions in all sectors, as well as by the contributions of SPPA alumni who are working in communities across the globe.[36]

The school's growing national recognition supported this self-assessment. At this time, *U.S. News & World Report* ranked SPPA thirty-seventh among 280 NASPAA-accredited programs, and a study conducted by the National Research Council ranked it twenty-third.[37]

In September 2014, an external review team[38] visited the school to complete the academic review process that had been commissioned by the University Faculty Senate. The review team's report described SPPA as being both in the top tier of public affairs schools and an important element of a first-tier research university. The team pointed especially to the role of the centers as the engines of the school's success, highlighting their contributions to the scholarship of engagement and the *Delaware Model* of public affairs education. The report also offered recommendations for strengthening the school's graduate and undergraduate programs and improving the integration of the programs. Overall, the team concluded that "the unit is resilient, and has done quite well under severe budgetary constraints. But further cuts to resources will likely mean changes to the core of the school's mission and programs." Their report called upon the university to better recognize that "nearly all the scholarly and research activity of a university has some reference in public policy, public management, and the broader public interest."[39] Within this context, the team endorsed the school's plan for hiring additional faculty to sustain and enhance its contributions as a comprehensive school of public affairs.

The external review team's report confirmed the value and importance of the school to the University of Delaware, and its recommendations laid out critical steps for the SPPA's future. The school concurred with the review team's overall assessment and committed to implementing its recommendations to strengthen integration across academic programs, adopt policies that clarified the roles of the centers, and infuse more content on American government institutions in the undergraduate programs.[40] However, neither the College of Arts and Sciences leadership nor the university administration formally responded to the external review team's report. The faculty hiring plan proposed by the school and supported by the external review team was not acted upon. As of the end of 2014, the School of Public Policy and Administration was a nationally ranked, comprehensive school of public affairs with more program responsibilities than ever before but without the faculty resources to sustain its development.

PART III

PURSUING THE NEW VISION

(2015–2021)

FIGURE 42. The inauguration of Dennis Assanis as the 28th President
of the University of Delaware on December 7, 2015, with Governor Jack Markell,
Joe Biden, Assanis, and Trustee Chair John Cochran.

CHAPTER SEVEN

RISING EXPECTATIONS

ON MARCH 2, 2015, University of Delaware President Patrick Harker announced that he would step down on June 30 to become president and chief executive officer of the Federal Research Bank of Philadelphia. On March 13, the Board of Trustees named a search committee to identify the university's next president and selected Nancy Targett, dean of the College of Earth, Ocean and Environment, to serve as acting president. Ultimately, on November 18, the board appointed Dennis Assanis as the twenty-eighth president of UD. Assanis was provost and senior vice president for academic affairs at Stony Brook University, a State University of New York campus.[1] He previously had served on the faculty of the University of Michigan and was familiar with the Gerald R. Ford School of Public Policy, which had moved to the top rank of public affairs schools after being named for the former president in 1999.

Soon after being appointed, Assanis reviewed the proposal previously developed for how UD would recognize Vice President Biden, which focused on creating a Biden Institute for Social Justice and Civic Engagement that would be housed in a new social sciences building. He determined that an alternative path should be considered. Assanis requested an analysis of how naming the School of Public Policy and Administration for Biden might advance an overall strategy to strengthen the school's national standing and build new alignments with other university academic units. He believed that the interdisciplinary character of a school of public policy could help advance new programs and partnerships on and beyond campus.[2]

Provost Domenico Grasso invited College of Arts and Sciences Dean George Watson to submit a white paper on the possibilities of naming the school for Biden and the likely effects of making the school a university priority. The task of writing the white paper fell to University Professor of Public Policy Dan Rich, and Senior Associate Dean for the Social Sciences David Wilson. The "White Paper: The Joseph R. Biden, Jr. School of Public Policy and Administration" was submitted on June 17, 2016.[3] Soon after, Assanis confirmed his support for the analysis and proposed action plan the paper articulated.

THE WHITE PAPER

The white paper described how naming the school for the forty-seventh Vice President of the United States could lead to the overall strengthening of the school and its programs: "Reflecting the Vice President's accomplishments and priorities, the Biden School will build upon SPPA's existing strengths, connect those strengths with other areas of university excellence, become the focal point for strategic investment, and rise rapidly to the top rankings of public affairs schools in the nation."[4] The paper detailed the resources needed to fulfill that vision. Most important was the addition of faculty lines, many of which should be at the senior level, targeted to core areas of public administration and public policy and areas of scholarship that would become increasingly recognized for excellence. Building upon its historical role, the Biden School would "be distinctive for providing research-driven, real-world solutions to the world's most challenging issues: improving education, community health, and environmental quality; encouraging economic innovation and prosperity; promoting equity, social justice, and cultural understanding; and strengthening services from all sectors to support a better and more secure quality of life."[5]

Rich and Wilson had reviewed the organizational models of prominent public affairs programs. They proposed that the Biden School should be a hybrid that combined some of the best features of leading schools with the distinctive strengths of UD's programs. This hybrid model would establish the Biden School as a hub for interdisciplinary policy programs around which there would be many spokes, each of which would represent partnerships with academic units across campus. The partnerships would bring together faculty, professionals, and students from many disciplines to collaborate on scholarly solutions to societal challenges. Initially, the Biden School would continue to reside within the social sciences portfolio of the College of Arts and Sciences. However, it was evident to Rich, Wilson, and Watson that, over the longer term, the Biden School should become a freestanding professional school parallel to its aspirational peers among the nation's leading schools of public affairs.

The white paper proposed that naming the school and establishing it as a university priority would immediately strengthen its stature. The key would be to effectively communicate these changes, particularly to leaders of the nation's public affairs programs who are primarily responsible for the ranking of programs.[6] National recognition would continue to grow as investments were made in hiring high-profile faculty in the core areas of public administration and public policy and in interdisciplinary fields where the school already had strengths.[7] The school would also offer special programs, some existing and some new, including creating the Biden Institute, which would focus on domestic policies. From the fall of 2016, President Assanis was outspoken in identifying the School of Public Policy and Administration as a priority. He was not hesitant to suggest that the school would be named for Biden.

THE BIDEN INSTITUTE

As the plan outlined in the white paper moved forward, university administrators discussed with Vice President Biden and his sister and key advisor Valerie Biden Owens the role that he and other senior members of the Biden team would play at the University of Delaware. Through the fall of 2016, an agreement was developed between the university and Biden that defined the terms of the new partnership. Biden was also in conversations with the University of Pennsylvania about a potential association. One question to be resolved was how his relationship with the two institutions would be differentiated.

On February 7, 2017, UD and Biden announced their new partnership, which would combine Vice President Biden's longtime work on domestic policy issues with the university's strengths in public policy education and research. Biden would serve as the founding chair of UD's Biden Institute, "a new research and policy center focused on developing public policy solutions on issues ranging from economic reform and environmental sustainability to civil rights, criminal justice, women's rights, and more. The Institute would also convene thought leaders on the most important issues of the day."[8] In a separate press release on that same day, the University of Pennsylvania announced that Biden had been named Benjamin Franklin Presidential Practice Professor and would lead the Penn Biden Center for Diplomacy and Global Engagement, which would be in Washington, DC.[9] The focus of the Penn Biden Center would be on international issues and challenges.

With a focus on domestic policy, UD's Biden Institute was conceived as a university-based think tank focused on the nation's most pressing problems. One of its primary roles would be to convene policy leaders, analysts, and advocates in an ongoing dialogue to define policy issues and evaluate options and do so in ways that would engage the entire UD campus and the wider community. Biden especially wanted a focus on expanding economic opportunity and social justice. Valerie Biden Owens became vice chair of the institute, and some of the individuals who had worked with Biden during his tenure as vice president joined the staff. Among them was Michael Donilon, who had been a senior advisor to Biden for virtually all of his political career. Donilon became managing director of the Biden Institute and joined the faculty of the School of Public Policy and Administration.

FIGURE 43. Michael Donilon, managing director, Biden Institute.

The Biden Institute's executive director, Catherine McLaughlin, previously served as executive director of the Institute of Politics at the John F. Kennedy School of Government at Harvard University. There, she attracted high-profile resident and visiting fellows and engaged university students in active dialogue with national and global political and policy leaders. She accepted the position

FIGURE 44. The Biden Institute, 44 Kent Way.

of executive director of the Biden Institute after resigning from Harvard to work for Secretary Hillary Clinton in the 2016 presidential election campaign. One of her priorities was for the institute to promote the value of civic engagement and encourage young people to enter public service and leadership positions. She also would encourage programs that highlighted political and policy debate.

The public launch of the Biden Institute came on April 7, 2017, when Biden addressed a crowd of 2,500 on the UD Green, with most of the students wearing "Biden is Back" T-shirts. Biden told the students he was proud of them because they wanted to change the world. He praised the School of Public Policy and Administration for providing the education needed to accomplish change. Biden shared his vision for the institute as "a world-class intellectual center" that would be a destination for leaders and scholars to visit from across the U.S. and around the world. And those visitors, he told students and faculty, "will be available to all of you" for discussions and other interactions.[10]

As soon as it was established, the Biden Institute initiated a series of campus programs with nationally known speakers, some of whom were invited to have public conversations with Biden on critical policy issues. The institute also launched programs for students to meet with political and policy leaders and, on many occasions, to meet and converse with Vice President Biden himself. Donilon became actively involved with UD's Washington, DC, semester, teaching and inviting well-known leaders to meet with its students. McLaughlin took advantage of her experience at Harvard to introduce programs, including a nonpartisan effort to increase voter registration among UD students, to help students recognize the responsibilities of citizenship. She also planned to build connections between civic engagement activities at UD and similar efforts at campuses across the nation.

FIGURE 45. Catherine McLaughlin, executive director, Biden Institute.

At Harvard, McLaughlin had worked closely with Valerie Biden Owens, a resident fellow at the Institute for Politics. McLaughlin proudly affirms that "politics has been her inspiration and composed her life's work."[11] Biden Owens also found her calling in politics. She led every campaign during her brother's political career before he became vice president, including his seven straight U.S. Senate victories and his unsuccessful runs for two Democratic presidential nominations. She also had been his principal surrogate on the campaign trail.[12] Biden Owens and McLaughlin both had extensive experience with and commitment to cultivating women's leadership in politics.

FIGURE 46. Biden is Back Rally, April 7, 2017.

FIGURE 47. Valerie Biden Owens receiving an honorary Doctor of Laws degree from John Cochran (left) and Dennis Assanis at the May 2018 commencement.

Indeed, Biden Owens had trained women worldwide to engage in and influence the political process. She worked extensively with Women's Campaign International in countries such as Liberia, Venezuela, Romania, and Taiwan, teaching women to organize and develop communication and political skills. She also served on the national board of the Women's Leadership Forum of the Democratic National Committee.

Biden Owens often attributes her leadership success to the confidence she developed as a student at UD. She reflected on her college experiences when she was the keynote speaker at the March 19, 2019, Women of Promise dinner. "UD gave me the freedom and the knowledge and the platform to nurture my confidence and to grow into myself and prove my brother right," Biden Owens said, referring to her brother Joe. "Confidence begins with conviction. You must find your own true north—the values that you stand for and the things that you simply cannot abide."[13] In recognition of her accomplishments, the university awarded Biden Owens an honorary Doctor of Laws degree in May 2018.

When Biden announced his third candidacy for the Democratic nomination for President of the United States on April 25, 2019, he resigned as chair of the Biden Institute. The institute continued its work as a research and policy center addressing some of the nation's key issues, particularly those affecting America's middle class. It also maintained programs that enabled UD faculty, staff, and students to meet with some of the nation's leading public officials and policy analysts. Some of these leaders were members of the institute's newly formed Policy Advisory Board. They included UD alumni David Plouffe, who had managed the 2008 Obama presidential campaign, and Steve Schmidt, who had managed the 2008 McCain presidential campaign. The chair of the Policy Advisory Board was Sarah Bianchi, former head of economic and domestic policy for Vice President Biden and global head of policy development for Airbnb. The board also included leaders from a wide range of sectors with expertise and experience related to key domestic policy priorities, especially the revitalization of the U.S. middle class.

Viewed in historical context, the establishment of the Biden Institute reaffirmed many of the values and commitments that had inspired the creation of the Division of Urban Affairs in 1961 and led to the establishment of centers and institutes in the various iterations of the school over the years. Like these earlier initiatives, the Biden Institute formed a bridge between the world of ideas and the world of action. It was dedicated to creating and applying knowledge to address some of the nation's central challenges and had an opportunity to influence the national policy agenda.

COMMUNITY ENGAGEMENT

The white paper had proposed that "civic engagement will be a central feature of the programs offered by the Biden School" and that "through civic engagement, students will become active citizens and recognize that what they learn in their classes can improve the communities where they live and work. The Biden School will help to make civic and community engagement a defining part of a UD education and prepare future generations of leaders dedicated to public and community service."[14] Civic and community engagement had been central to the School of Public Policy and Administration's identity from its inception and was built into the *Delaware Model* of public affairs education. In 2016, another institutional dimension was added, the Community Engagement Initiative (CEI).

CEI came about from a grassroots effort of faculty, staff, and students in 2014 to assemble a successful application for the Community Engagement Classification from the Carnegie Foundation for the Advancement of Teaching.[15] The classification underscored the university's role as a dynamic force for incorporating engagement in the education of its students and the scholarship of its faculty. In February 2016, Provost Domenico Grasso launched the Community Engagement Initiative to further strengthen UD's identity as an engaged university. Although it was a unit of the provost's office, CEI was housed in SPPA, where CEI Director Dan Rich had his faculty appointment. Deputy Director Lynnette Overby, a professor of dance and the lead architect for the University of Delaware's Carnegie Classification, had a joint appointment in the school. CEI and the school were to become partners in efforts to strengthen civic and community engagement across campus and in the communities the university served. Maria Aristigueta points out that this partnership was mutually beneficial and that "the symbolic placement of the Community Engagement Initiative in Graham Hall speaks to the important contributions that the school makes to community engagement."[16]

In fall 2016, as the Biden Institute was coming together, President Assanis agreed to join other university presidents in meeting a challenge posed by Campus Compact, a national organization of approximately twelve hundred higher education institutions committed to civic and community engagement. The organization had called upon presidents of member universities to develop civic action plans representing their institutions' strategic plans for enhancing community engagement.[17] The UD Civic Action Plan was completed in the fall of 2017. Assanis approved it and submitted it to Campus Compact in December 2017. Summarizing the plan, he explained, "The University of Delaware Civic Action Plan articulates our strategic vision and sets the agenda to strengthen our contributions as one of the nation's most engaged research universities. While the university is proud of its Community Engagement Classification from the Carnegie Foundation, we consider it not so much an achievement but a starting point."[18]

Over the next three years, most of the recommendations of the Civic Action Plan were implemented.[19] All seven deans defined their college's commitments and contributions to community engagement in alignment with their overall priorities. A university-wide Council on Community Engagement actively promoted policies and practices that supported collaborative initiatives across campus and in the communities that UD serves.[20] In May 2018, the University Faculty Senate approved the Community Engagement Scholars course of study, the first university-wide undergraduate course of study available to all undergraduates in all colleges. By fall 2019, 115 students were enrolled. Under this program, thirteen CEI faculty fellows carried out engaged scholarship projects in the community and two dozen more faculty fellows participated in CEI partnerships. In May 2019, the Faculty Senate presented the first faculty awards for excellence in engaged scholarship and approved a graduate certificate in Engaged Scholarship.[21] The following year, it presented the first university-wide graduate student awards for excellence in engaged scholarship.[22]

The Civic Action Plan called for creating five new knowledge-based community partnerships. These were designed to mobilize university-wide capacity in areas of community priority. All the partnerships drew upon the contributions of faculty, professionals, and students from the School of Public Policy and Administration. First, the Partnership for Public Education, which had already launched in the fall of 2016, was a product of the school's work on issues of educational equity and was designed to mobilize university-wide resources to improve Delaware public education.[23] It was led by Liz Farley-Ripple, a faculty member in the School of Education who had a joint appointment in the SPPA, and by colleagues from IPA.

The Partnership for Healthy Communities (PHC) was launched on October 30, 2017, at an event with Joe Biden as the featured speaker. The purpose of PHC was to mobilize UD's capacity to find ways to improve the health and well-being of Delaware residents, particularly those living in communities characterized by social and economic disadvantage. PHC was led by former Delaware Secretary of Health and Social Services Rita Landgraf, professor of practice in the College of Health Sciences, and Erin Knight (PhD, UAPP 2011), a faculty member in SPPA and associate director of its Center for Community Research and Service.[24]

In fall 2017, President Assanis and Delaware State University President Harry Williams signed an agreement with Wilmington Mayor Mike Purzycki to create the Wilmington Policy Partnership, the first formal framework for a university collaboration with the city since the Wilmington Community Development Partnership in the 1990s. Parallel to this effort, the Center for Community and Research Service supported an effort to coordinate the contributions of the many UD units that offer programs and services in Wilmington by facilitating periodic meetings between the leaders of those programs to promote collaboration and new initiatives.

The Partnership for Arts and Culture (PAC), led by Lynnette Overby, was launched on March 10, 2018. The partnership engaged representatives from seventy university and community arts and culture organizations to support collaborations to strengthen arts and cultural institutions at all levels, local to global. With funding generated from the university and community partners,

FIGURE 48. Lynnette Overby, director of the Community Engagement Initiative, June 2021.

FIGURE 49. Provost Robin Morgan speaks at the first Provost's Symposium on Engaged Scholarship, March 5, 2020.

PAC supported a small grants program that funded collaborative projects to expand the role of arts and culture in communities throughout Delaware and beyond.

Finally, in UD's home community of Newark, the Community Engagement Initiative and the Institute for Public Administration provided start-up support for The Newark Partnership (TNP), a city-wide, community-based nonprofit organization dedicated to the city's economic, social, aesthetic, and environmental enhancement. TNP was incorporated on December 30, 2018, and focused on growing the city's economic prosperity, strengthening the contributions of Newark's nonprofit sector, and promoting civic engagement on issues of importance to the city's future.[25]

Another program established as part of the university's commitment to civic engagement was the annual Provost's Symposium on Engaged Scholarship, the first of which was held on March 5, 2020. Hosted by Provost Robin Morgan, the symposium brought together 150 UD faculty and professionals, and the deans of all the colleges, to develop priorities for enhancing engaged scholarship.[26] A year later, Morgan announced that Lynnette Overby would become director of the Community Engagement Initiative upon the retirement of Dan Rich on May 31, 2021.[27]

WHAT'S IN A NAME?

By fall 2017, some of the action steps described in the white paper were clearly being implemented. Most importantly, the faculty hiring plan was proceeding. Sebastian Jannelli from the Office of Development and Alumni Relations was assigned to focus on fundraising for a new building that would be named Biden Hall. He later became the development officer for the Biden School. While the focus of the building plan before Assanis's arrival had been on a consolidated social science building with a Biden Institute for Social Justice and Civic Engagement, the newer plan was to have the building house the Biden School and the Biden Institute. For some, however, the relationship between the Biden Institute and the Biden School was somewhat perplexing. The Biden Institute had been created, but the school had not been named. As a result, some of the benefits expected from the school's naming were delayed.

In part to help raise the profile of Biden's new partnership with the University of Delaware and boost recognition of the School of Public Policy and Administration, Biden was the featured speaker at the October 2017 national conference of the Network of Schools of Public Policy, Affairs and Administration (NASPAA). He encouraged the over three hundred educators and administrators there to help students become, and remain, engaged in public policy and public service. He shared his deep concern about the decline of the American middle class. Biden issued a challenge to the assembled leaders of public affairs programs: "What policy solutions do you propose to ensure America has a growing and thriving middle class?"[28] He asked them to engage themselves and their colleagues in developing those solutions, and invited all of them to reconvene at the UD the following year. At a reception hosted by the university in conjunction with the conference, Assanis described the importance of the new partnership between UD and the Vice President. He also shared the open secret that, sometime in the future, the School of Public Policy and Administration would be named for Biden.[29]

On September 28, 2018, the follow-up conference Biden had called for, the Biden Challenge conference on revitalizing the middle class, was held on the UD campus. Organized by the Biden Institute and SPPA, participants included many who had heard Biden issue his challenge a year earlier. They also included policy leaders from across the U.S. The conference included panel discussions and idea exchanges on policies and issues affecting the sustainability of the middle class.[30] Attendees at the conference were told that the school would be named for Biden, but no timeline was confirmed.[31]

When George Watson, who had been dean of the College of Arts and Sciences for more than a decade, retired at the end of the summer of 2018, Associate Dean John Pelesko succeeded him.[32] Pelesko, like Watson, was an active supporter of plans for the Biden School. President Assanis continued to designate the development of the school as a priority. Encouragement to move ahead with the naming came a month after the Biden Challenge conference. Sandra Archibald, dean of the Evans School of Public Policy and Governance at the University of Washington, visited UD as the Charles P. Messick Visiting Scholar. Archibald had been dean at Evans since 2003 and had been responsible for changing the trajectory of that school. At one point, the very existence of the Evans School had been challenged. Archibald not only saved the school but then led it into the top rank of public affairs programs in the nation. Archibald was quite familiar with UD's School of Public Policy and Administration and had worked with many of its faculty through NASPAA and ASPA. The title for her presentation, which was organized as an interview with SPPA Director Aristigueta, was "Why Am I Jealous of Delaware? Innovations, Programs, and Initiatives of Top Ten Schools." President Assanis and Provost Morgan attended her presentation, along with other senior UD administrators and CAS Dean Pelesko.

Archibald was unequivocal that SPPA had a solid foundation and was in a far better position to move rapidly into the top rank of the nation's public affairs programs than the Evans School had been when she became dean. She explained the reasons for her assessment and what she thought was required for UD to take advantage of the opportunity to raise its profile. Two points were clear. First, the school needed to be named for Biden without further delay. Second, it needed to become a freestanding, independent professional school of public affairs led by a dean, comparable to its aspirational peers. That was the accepted and expected model for public affairs schools nationally, and until that model was implemented at UD, its school would not have the recognition it deserved.[33]

FIGURE 50. Joe Biden speaks at the Biden Challenge conference,
Clayton Hall, September 28, 2018.

Of course, another factor in the timing of the school's naming was that Biden was expected to decide about running for U.S. President early in 2019. It would be complicated to add his name to the school once he was an active candidate. This recognition provided additional impetus to move ahead.

Assanis announced the establishment of the Joseph R. Biden, Jr. School of Public Policy and Administration at the December 11, 2018, UD Board of Trustees meeting. Aristigueta, expressing the views held by her colleagues, projected the impact of the action taken:[34] "The newly named Biden School is poised to build upon our existing strengths to become a globally recognized, comprehensive school of public affairs that offers outstanding academics and conducts interdisciplinary research into solutions for some of the world's greatest challenges. Along with substantive policy research, the Biden School's programs will help to make civic and community engagement a defining part of a UD education and prepare future generations of leaders, scholars, and researchers dedicated to meeting critical societal needs."[35]

On February 26, 2019, a celebration of the naming of the Biden School took place at Clayton Hall. Assanis noted the historical significance of the moment, not only for the school but also for the university: "Few institutions are fortunate enough to be able to claim as an alumnus a leader and public servant as distinguished as Joe Biden . . . By affixing the Biden name to the essential work being done here, we are reaffirming our commitment to integrity, to service and to excellence." Biden described himself as "humbled and honored by the renaming of the school" and praised professors who, he said, gave him the confidence to believe that he could make a difference in the world. "I owe this university a great deal," he said. "I hope the Biden School can convince a new generation of women and men that they can make a difference."[36]

The celebration featured a conversation between Biden and Pulitzer Prize-winning presidential historian Jon Meacham that focused on themes from Meacham's book *The Soul of America: The Battle for Our Better Angels.*[37] Toward the conclusion of the discussion, Meacham posed the question to Biden that was on the minds of most of those in the audience: "Will you become a candidate for President in 2020?" Biden responded that he was "in the final stages of [making] that decision." "They—the most important people in my life—want me to run," he explained, describing the consensus expressed at a recent family meeting. But, he said, he was still exploring the details of what it would take to put a campaign together and considering whether to proceed.

POLITICS

Joe Biden's announcement of his candidacy for U.S. President on April 25, 2019, generated understandable excitement across the University of Delaware campus, particularly in the school that was named for him only months before. Many members of the UD community looked forward to

FIGURE 51. John Cochran, Valerie Biden Owens, Joe and Jill Biden, and Eleni and Dennis Assanis at the Biden School Naming reception, Clayton Hall, February 26, 2019.

FIGURE 52. Joe Biden and Jon Meacham at the Biden School naming event, Clayton Hall, February 26, 2019.

actively supporting the candidacy of its most famous alumnus. However, the university as an institution would remain nonpartisan, as required by its charter and confirmed by its policy.[38] Maintaining that institutional distance was more complicated than it had been in earlier campaigns because Biden now had a more formal association with the university, and that association was a well-publicized point of institutional pride.[39] After Biden's announcement as a candidate, the university leadership reminded the campus community about university policies on political activity.[40]

During the primaries, the university was not drawn into the campaign other than by the quite welcome recognition of UD as Biden's alma mater. There was occasional recognition that the school of public policy and administration had been named for him and that the Biden Institute included key advisors of his, most notably Valerie Biden Owens and Michael Donilon.[41] The university's Office of Communication and Marketing navigated media inquiries as the campaign moved forward. At times, individuals at the Biden School and the Biden Institute were contacted by people looking for a channel to the Biden campaign. All of those cases were deferred with replies that UD was not a conduit to the campaign.

While the policies were clear and consistent, the evolving situation with the campaign eventually entangled the university in political controversy. In April 2020, a dispute arose around Biden's senatorial papers, which had been donated to the University of Delaware Library in 2012. The university received numerous Freedom of Information Act (FOIA) requests for records relating to an alleged sexual harassment complaint, but they were all denied.[42] The decision not to release the papers was based on two principles. First, such a release could only occur with the donor's approval, in compliance with the donation agreement between Biden and the university. Biden had not authorized the release of the papers.[43] Second, FOIA did not apply to the university if no state funds were used to obtain the items requested or if they did not relate to meetings of the Board of Trustees. No state funds had been used to obtain the Biden senatorial papers.

After it received further complaints regarding the release of the papers, the university's interpretation of FOIA limits in reference to the requested items was submitted for review to the Office of the Delaware Attorney General. In two separate opinions, the office held that UD had not violated FOIA with respect to the denial of the records request submitted. Those opinions were appealed to the Delaware State Superior Court.[44] On January 4, 2021, the Superior Court rejected both appeals and affirmed the attorney general's conclusion that UD was not in violation of FOIA.[45] The controversy over the senatorial papers highlighted the unavoidable fact that the welcome notoriety that the university received for its proud association with Biden might sometimes be accompanied by public criticism.

On December 2, 2020, shortly after Biden was elected, the Office of General Counsel issued a new, updated university policy on political activity and lobbying. It reaffirmed the non-partisan requirements under the university charter and the lobbying limits consistent with its status as a tax-exempt nonprofit institution. On January 20, 2021, Joseph Robinette Biden, Jr., was sworn in as the Forty-Sixth President of the United States, with his hand on a family Bible held by Dr. Jill Biden, another proud Blue Hen.

President Biden called on several UD alumni with ties to the Biden School to help launch his administration. Michael Donilon, former managing director of the Biden Institute, was appointed senior White House advisor, and others affiliated with the institute also joined the administration.[46] Delaware's U.S. Congressional Representative Lisà Blunt Rochester (MA, UAPP 2002) served as co-chair of the Presidential Inaugural Committee and on the vetting committee for the vice presidential selection. Tony Allen, who had worked on Biden's staff in the 1990s and was president of Delaware State University, was appointed co-chair of the Presidential Inaugural Committee. Cecilia Martinez (PhD, UAPP 1990), a former research associate in the Center for Energy and Environmental Policy, served as part of the Biden-Harris Transition Team and was appointed senior director for environmental justice for the White House Council on Environmental Quality.[47]

AN INDEPENDENT SCHOOL

Once the school was named for Biden, the University of Delaware leadership shifted its attention to establishing it as a freestanding professional school. This action was more than a technical, administrative change in the school's identity. UD, unlike most other research universities, had no freestanding professional schools. Becoming freestanding would mean that the school would be led by a dean who reported directly to the provost. The heads of all other UD schools reported to a college dean.

On September 6, 2019, Provost Morgan and College of Arts and Sciences Dean Pelesko met with the Biden School faculty to confirm that they would be receptive to a faculty recommendation that the school become a freestanding unit. Morgan also indicated that she was ready to initiate a national search for the school's dean once the decision process had moved through the University Faculty Senate. On October 4, the Biden School faculty, with the support of school director Maria Aristigueta, voted to recommend becoming a freestanding professional school led by a dean effective July 1, 2020.[48] The faculty argued that this change would significantly strengthen the school, placing it at a level in the university comparable to that of the nation's other leading public affairs schools.

On October 21, 2019, the Biden School faculty's recommendation was presented by Dean Pelesko for discussion at the College of Arts and Sciences Faculty Senate.[49] This meeting was preliminary to the University Faculty Senate's consideration. The process should have moved forward without complications, given the support of the school's faculty and the endorsement of college and university administration. However, that was not the case.

Some of the complications were procedural and reflected concerns about the rapid timetable for the decision rather than the proposal's merits. Other questions concerned the implications of the decision for the university's academic structure.

A year earlier, a new graduate college had been approved with a very different composition from the existing colleges. In addition, at the same time as the Biden School transition was being considered, a proposal was initiated to convert the UD Honors Program to an honors college. Most significantly, creating a freestanding professional school was at variance with the prevailing university organization in which all schools were parts of colleges.[50] The Biden School proposal raised questions about the status of the other schools and whether they would remain in their current colleges or would become freestanding, and if so, based on what criteria. Just two weeks before the CAS Faculty Senate's consideration of the Biden School proposal, the University Faculty Senate had approved a proposal for the Department of Music to become the School of Music, but with the specific provision that it would remain in the College of Arts and Sciences. However, after considerable discussion and a failed proposal to defer the decision, the CAS Faculty Senate approved the Biden School's transition proposal.[51]

As the Biden School proposal moved to the University Faculty Senate, it was apparent that the proposal needed to be subjected to the complete review process typically required for senate action. That meant a change in the previously anticipated timetable. A vote was not expected on the Biden School becoming a freestanding professional school until late in the spring semester of 2020. Provost Morgan confirmed that she would not initiate a search for the dean of the Biden School until the Faculty Senate acted.

Senate President Matt Robinson recommended that, before the Biden School and other organizational proposals were considered, the Faculty Senate should have an open discussion on the overall academic structure of the university, and the difference between a school, a college, and a department. At an open discussion on December 9, 2019, Robinson pointed out that four current schools had previously been freestanding colleges led by a dean, including the Biden School, the School of Marine Studies, the School of Education, and the School of Nursing.[52] Further, most research universities have a mix of both colleges and professional schools led by deans and operating at the same administrative level as colleges. UD was the exception.

In February 2020, Aristigueta sent a detailed report to the Faculty Senate entitled "The Biden School's Transition to a Freestanding Professional School." The report presented the case for the transition and provided detailed documentation to support that case, including the argument that eighteen of the twenty top public affairs programs in the nation were freestanding schools led by a dean. In fact, virtually all of the nation's leading public affairs schools were independent units that became magnets for development opportunities and broader partnerships with institutions from all sectors, local to global. The report proposed that a freestanding Biden School would have similar benefits for the University of Delaware. The school's independence would enable it to better support the distinctive features of its professional culture and its role in public service and applied research, all of which had documented importance for its success. The report concluded, "the Biden School's transition will better support its mission, programs, and people; increase its contributions across the campus and in the wider community, and enhance national recognition for its programs and the University of Delaware."[53]

In late February and early March, the proposal was considered by the Senate Committees on Undergraduate Studies, Graduate Studies, and Budget and by the Senate Coordinating Committee. All of them endorsed the proposal. On Monday, April 6, the University Faculty Senate convened remotely, as the campus had closed due to the Coronavirus health crisis. The last item on the agenda was a vote on freestanding status for the Biden School. The senate voted by a large margin to approve the resolution.[54] The Board of Trustees subsequently approved the change. Effective July 1, 2020, the Joseph R. Biden, Jr. School of Public Policy and Administration became the first freestanding professional school at the University of Delaware.

CHAPTER EIGHT

THE BIDEN SCHOOL

THE SCHOOL OF PUBLIC POLICY AND ADMINISTRATION had been on a growth trajectory as a result of the new vision Assanis announced for its development in 2015. Even before SPPA was officially renamed the Biden School, new faculty positions were approved that aligned with the priorities described in Dan Rich and David Wilson's 2016 white paper. The faculty increased from twenty-four in 2014 to thirty-five in 2019, with additional faculty positions committed as part of the approved hiring plan. The number of joint-appointment faculty increased when the school expanded its collaborative programs with other academic units. Scholars from policy analysis, public administration, and urban affairs were joined by colleagues in engineering, physics, law, geography, philosophy, public health, environmental science, and education.

Upon being named the Biden School, its four previously affiliated centers and institutes—the Center for Applied Demography and Survey Research, Center for Community Research and Service, Center for Historic Architecture and Design, and Institute for Public Administration—were joined by the Biden Institute and the Center for Energy and Environmental Policy. Two additional units were also affiliated with the school: the Disaster Research Center and the Community Engagement Initiative.[1] Each of the new units expanded the scope of the school's programs and engaged the participation of additional faculty, professionals, and students.

GROWTH OF THE ACADEMIC PROGRAMS

The new faculty hired after 2015 expanded the scope of the school's interdisciplinary research and strengthened its academic programs. They also increased capacity in the core areas of public policy and public administration and substantive areas of education policy, health policy, energy and environmental policy, and disaster science and management.[2] Many of the veteran faculty were also engaged in emerging policy research areas.[3]

Equally important, some new faculty took on leadership positions in the expanding graduate programs. Sarah Bruch became director of the PhD in Urban Affairs and Public Policy, and the program was renamed the PhD in Public Policy and Administration to align with the name of the school.

FIGURE 53. The Biden School's new name is displayed
on a banner at the entrance to Graham Hall.

FIGURE 54. Joe Biden with members of the Biden School faculty
after the naming of the school, December 11, 2018.

FIGURE 55A Sarah Bruch, director of the PhD in Public Policy and Administration;
FIGURE 55B Katie Fitzpatrick, director of the Master of Public Policy program; and,
FIGURE 55C Daniel Smith, director of the MPA program.

Katie Fitzpatrick led the newly launched Master of Public Policy program, one of the essential degrees for a comprehensive school of public affairs. Kimberley Isett led the policy side of the new Master of Public Health (MPH), jointly offered with the College of Health Sciences. Daniel Smith directed the MPA program until he was appointed associate dean for the social sciences in the College of Arts and Sciences in July 2021.

Other graduate leadership roles were filled by veteran faculty. Joseph Trainor, who was leading the Disaster Science and Management graduate program, became the school's director of doctoral studies, overseeing the coordinated development of its PhD programs. Ismat Shah, a materials science and engineering professor with a joint appointment in the school, directed the energy and environmental policy graduate program. Danilo Yanich continued to serve as director of the MA in Urban Affairs and Public Policy, a position he held since 2006.

The MPA program developed an online option to serve part-time students recruited nationally through a partnership with Wiley, one of the nation's leading online services platforms. Maria Aristigueta recalls several meetings with Wiley's representatives, who suggested that there might be significant demand for an online MPA program. She explains, "I embraced that option because the school needed to draw paying professional master's students, and we had not experienced much success bringing part-time students to campus. The commitment was made to have the full-time Biden School faculty develop and teach the courses, thereby maintaining the quality of the program and meeting accreditation requirements."[4]

The online MPA and other new programs significantly impacted the School of Public Policy and Administration's masters-level enrollment. Master's degree enrollment had declined through 2015, but it rebounded and increased by 2019. The scholarship program approved by Dean George Watson in 2015 reduced the cost of tuition for Delawareans and those working in the public and nonprofit sectors. In March 2021, the University of Delaware trustees reduced graduate tuition in the school and other units by 50 percent, bringing it in line with rates at peer institutions. Among other factors, this increased fall 2021 enrollment in the Biden School's master's degree programs and raised total graduate enrollment to two hundred.

While the school had been oriented toward graduate programs for much of its history, by 2019, it offered undergraduate majors and minors in Organizational and Community Leadership, Public Policy, and Energy and Environmental Policy, as well as a minor in Public Health (offered jointly with the College of Health Sciences).[5] The number of undergraduates increased steadily and dramatically, from 110 majors and minors in 2009 to 569 majors and minors in 2019. While most of the school's faculty taught undergraduates in addition to graduates, some focused mainly on the undergraduate programs.

FIGURE 56. Danilo Yanich (PhD 1980), professor (1985–2021) and director of the MA in Urban Affairs and Public Policy, with research assistants Allison Becker (MA 2015) and David Karas (PhD 2017).

FIGURE 57A Karen Stein (PhD, 1984), director, Leadership Program, 2005–9, and director, Organizational and Community Leadership Program, 2010–21; and FIGURE 57B Breck Robinson, director, undergraduate Public Policy Program, 2015–21.

This focus was particularly true for the faculty working with the Organizational and Community Leadership program, which had been the first undergraduate program in the school in 2004. Karen Stein continued to serve as program director, working with James L. Morrison, Anthony Middlebrooks, and Jane Case Lilly (PhD, UAPP 2008).

As the Public Policy major grew, more of the school's faculty played a role in that program. Breck Robinson served as program director from 2015 to 2021, and Nina David, Erin Knight, Andrea Pierce, and Philip Barnes played central roles in instruction and advisement. In addition, doctoral students served as teaching assistants and course instructors, which provided those students with funding support and experience in teaching and student advising, and supplemented the undergraduate teaching capacity.

By 2019, excellence and innovation in undergraduate education had become part of the institutional signature of the Biden School. Perhaps one of the best examples of this was the establishment of 4+1 options for highly qualified Public Policy, Organizational and Community Leadership, and Energy and Environmental Policy undergraduates.[6] By 2021, a dozen 4+1 programs enabled undergraduates in majors as diverse as English, Economics, and Women's Studies to complete one of the Biden School's master's programs on an accelerated schedule.

THE COVID-19 CRISIS

To some extent, the immediate impact of the Biden School's transition was overshadowed by the challenges of the COVID-19 health crisis. For the University of Delaware and the Biden School, like other educational institutions, the year 2020 was unsettling, fraught with uncertainties, different from any time in the past, and ultimately transformative. The crisis unfolded in a series of waves, beginning with a sudden and almost total transition to online instruction in the spring semester and extending to a series of budget cuts and personnel actions that grew in scale and consequence through the fall.[7] The campus closed in mid-March and remained closed for the remainder of 2020 and through the spring and summer of 2021. The dominant medium of university life became videoconferencing on Zoom. The new motto for the entire Blue Hen community became "Protect the Flock!"

On April 27, 2020, President Assanis sent a message to the UD community summarizing the university's response to the evolving crisis and its fiscal consequences and indicating that, for the spring semester, the unforeseen impact on the campus budget was calculated to be more than $65 million. The university administration adopted a series of cost-cutting and efficiency measures to address these budget impacts, including an immediate university-wide hiring freeze, a travel ban, a deferral of some previously approved capital projects, a moratorium on approval of new projects, a suspension of discretionary spending, and staff realignments to support greater efficiency.

In this turbulent and unprecedented environment, the Biden School's transition proceeded, mainly on schedule, but under circumstances quite different than previously anticipated. The hiring freeze indefinitely suspended the school's approved faculty hiring plan. The additional professional staff needed to support the operation of a freestanding school would not be hired for the foreseeable future. The crisis also created practical challenges for the school's applied research and public service programs, particularly those that required active engagement with external institutions. Faculty, staff, and students alike faced immediate challenges to carrying out their research, including dissertation research that required travel or the gathering of data directly from the wider community. Many scrambled to revise their research designs to accommodate the limits posed by the pandemic.

As of July 1, 2020, when the Biden School became a freestanding unit, UD's fiscal situation was still in flux, and no units had confirmed budgets for the new fiscal year. The university was implementing a new budgeting model before the onset of the health crisis, and some of its details had still not been confirmed. The Biden School faced the additional complication that it was transitioning from a budget that had been part of the College of Arts and Sciences to one that was independent.

The fall 2020 semester began on September 1, almost entirely online. By then, the fiscal forecast for UD had worsened. Assanis announced further actions to mitigate the budget shortfall.[8] UD would not resume primarily in-person instruction and other operations until the opening of the fall 2021 semester.[9]

IMPLEMENTING THE SCHOOL'S TRANSITION

Despite the COVID-19 crisis, the Biden School's position as an important pillar of the University of Delaware's future had not changed. Even so, the crisis changed many plans, including the school's leadership plan. By 2018, Maria Aristigueta had served two five-year terms as the School for Public Policy and Administration's director and, at the request of President Assanis, agreed to stay on for two additional years to facilitate the transition to a freestanding Biden School. In September 2019, when Provost Robin Morgan met with the faculty to discuss the prospect of that transition, she expressed her intention to initiate a national search for the dean of the Biden School as soon as the University Faculty Senate confirmed its support for the transition. However, in May 2020, after the public health crisis gripped the campus and a hiring freeze was put in place, Morgan confirmed to the school's faculty that a national search was not feasible and that an interim dean would be appointed. To expedite the selection process, she solicited nominations, including self-nominations from the faculty.

FIGURE 58. Maria Aristigueta appointed Dean of the Joseph R. Biden, Jr. School of Public Policy and Administration, August 15, 2020.

After the nomination process was completed and a few candidates were interviewed, Morgan told the school's faculty that the selection process had demonstrated very strong support for Aristigueta. On August 13, after confirmation by the Board of Trustees, President Assanis and Provost Morgan announced the appointment of Aristigueta as the founding dean of the Biden School. The "interim" notation was dropped.[10]

Dean Aristigueta's first act was to gain approval from Provost Morgan to fill out the school's leadership team with the appointment of two associate deans: Kimberley Isett and Joseph Trainor.[11] Both faculty members were already playing key leadership roles. Isett had facilitated the review process for the school's transition plan, led the policy track for the new Master of Public Health program, and worked on initiatives to increase faculty research productivity. Trainor had been director of the Disaster Science and Management graduate program and served as the school's director of doctoral studies. Isett was appointed associate dean for research, and Trainor was appointed associate dean for academic affairs. The fourth member of the school's central administrative leadership team was Nicole Quinn, senior business manager. Her role was expanding in line with the Biden School's transition to freestanding status, particularly as college-level financial, human resources, and other operational responsibilities were now the school's direct responsibility.

With the support of the faculty, Aristigueta confirmed to Morgan that the top priority for the school was to implement its transition effectively. That translated into developing new school policies, plans, and practices, enhancing undergraduate and graduate student services, implementing a new model for graduate student funding, and changing some of the operating guidelines for the school's centers. All this was to be achieved despite the impacts of the COVID-19 crisis. The school's leadership team was also charged with improving scholarship and research output, promoting greater external recognition, and developing new collaborative programs with other academic units.

The relationship between the Biden Institute and the school was clarified during the transition. The institute was to be fully integrated as a unit of the school. One immediate sign of the benefits of that integration was the support that the Biden Institute staff provided to the school, which was even more critical in the environment of resource scarcity resulting from the pandemic.[12] The institute's integration with the school was also reflected in Aristigueta's invitation to its vice chair Valerie Biden Owens to be a member of the school's Board of Advisors and reliance on institute Executive Director Catherine McLaughlin to help restructure the board.[13]

As the school's transition progressed, another external issue affecting the entire university and the nation besides COVID-19 commanded attention. Growing societal demands for racial justice in the wake of the killing

FIGURE 59A Kimberley Isett, Associate Dean for Research; **FIGURE 59B** Joseph Trainor, Associate Dean for Academic Affairs; and **FIGURE 59**, Nicole Quinn, Senior Business Manager.

of George Floyd and other African Americans focused the attention of faculty, staff, and students on what the university should be doing to promote equity, diversity, and inclusion in its own operations and in the community. President Assanis already had identified inclusive excellence and increasing student and faculty diversity as UD priorities. Now there were growing expectations of the university to act more aggressively in those areas.

Diversity has been a priority of the Biden School's identity in its various iterations since its inception. However, some school faculty, staff, and students felt that it had not been a high priority in more recent years and that the school needed to reestablish its leadership role in that area. A town hall dialogue sponsored by Aristigueta in the summer of 2020 identified a series of issues to be addressed, including concerns about a lack of sustained efforts to recruit, support, and retain students, staff, and faculty of diverse backgrounds and insufficient consideration of equity issues and racial justice in the school's academic programs.[14] In July, Aristigueta established an informal working group to examine the issues raised.[15] With the support of the faculty, she also revived a standing committee on diversity, with faculty member Nina David as chair.[16] Aristigueta planned to work with that committee to implement recommendations for action and monitor ongoing progress.[17] The school joined the Community Engagement Initiative and other units in sponsoring a year-long speaker series on racial justice that focused on opportunities to enhance the university's support for inclusion and diversity through community engagement. The series became the focal point for a grassroots, university-wide initiative on antiracism that attracted faculty, staff, and students.[18]

In December 2020, the Biden School working group issued an interim report that outlined areas for strengthening diversity, equity, and inclusion (DEI). A key theme of the interim report was the need to institutionalize increased and ongoing support for DEI across the school's programs and policies. Though the report projected the submission of final recommendations by the end of the academic year, the working group was disbanded before submitting those recommendations and the responsibility for pursuing DEI initiatives then fell to a revived standing committee working with the dean. The standing committee subsequently proposed two new initiatives: the creation of a Biden School summer institute to recruit and support diverse undergraduate and graduate students, and the provision of funding for faculty and graduate students of color to undertake innovative, interdisciplinary scholarship related to core issues of equity, diversity, and inclusion. Both initiatives were supported by Dean Aristigueta and endorsed by the UD Office of Institutional Equity, Diversity and Inclusion. As of the end of 2021, the school had not yet obtained funding for these initiatives.[19] Even so, one sign of the renewed commitment to diversity and inclusion was the faculty's decision at its December meeting to eliminate the Graduate Record Examination (GRE) as an admissions requirement for all Biden School graduate programs. The decision was based on the faculty's view that GRE scores are not a reliable indicator of the ability of students to succeed in their graduate programs and that the exam discriminates against both minority and mid-career applicants.[20]

BIDEN HALL

The fall 2021 semester marked a return to on-campus instruction and a resumption of most in-person operations. The university mandated vaccinations for students, faculty, and staff with other provisions instituted to maintain health and safety. Despite the impacts of the COVID-19 crisis, fundraising efforts for the Biden School continued, including a sustained campaign to generate funding for the new building that would house the Biden School and Biden Institute and eventually become Biden Hall.

The plan for the new building, originally conceived in 2010, had evolved and changed many times over the subsequent decade. When the school was named for Biden, it was confirmed that the Biden School would anchor the building. As conceived, Biden Hall would enable the school to grow and become "an interdisciplinary intellectual hub to convene students, faculty, leaders, practitioners, and community members from a diverse range of disciplines, political ideologies, and sociocultural-economic backgrounds all under one roof."[21] The new building would occupy the last remaining plot of land on the university's historic Green, next to the Morris Library. The school would move from its current home, a former public elementary school built in the 1940s, to what was described in the fundraising proposal as "a grand Georgian-style building that will stand proudly on our campus for many centuries to come."[22] The school's location in the new building would reinforce its identity as a freestanding professional school and provide the programming space needed to carry out key activities in support of the school's and the university's priorities, including public programs undertaken by the Biden Institute featuring major national and global figures.

CIVIC ENGAGEMENT AND CIVIL DISCOURSE

From the outset, the Biden Institute focused on promoting civic engagement and civic discourse in the national political dialogue. It sponsored events and programs featuring political and policy leaders who approached issues from diverse perspectives. On October 17, 2017, Vice President Biden led an event entitled "Bridging the Divides," cosponsored by the Biden Institute and the Center for Political Communication. The event featured a conversation between Biden and Ohio's Republican governor John Kasich about the value of political cooperation and consensus. They agreed that the increasing polarization of political discourse threatened the democratic system. "The system itself has been breaking down on base politics," Kasich said. "The whole system is polarizing." Biden warned that it is "not possible

FIGURE 60. Student Volunteers at the National Voter Registration Day
program on the Green, September 24, 2019.

for this country to function without reaching a consensus."[23] The Biden Institute also was committed to increasing University of Delaware students' civic engagement, particularly by encouraging their participation in the democratic process and informing them on policy issues. One of its programs was sponsoring a voter registration drive that engaged UD student volunteers.

The school's work in civic engagement and civil discourse had begun with the creation of the Democracy Project, an Institute for Public Administration program initiated in 1998 that remained active when the Biden School became freestanding. Designed as a summer professional development institute for teachers, the program was cosponsored by the Delaware Office of the Secretary of State and the Delaware Heritage Commission. Joe Biden and his staff have been regular participants in the project over the years.[24] Participating teachers meet with public officials to learn about the workings of government and gain practical knowledge, including how to create lesson plans for teaching civics. After two decades, over four hundred Delaware teachers have participated in the program.

In addition to spearheading the summer institute, the leaders of the Democracy Project, Ed Freel and Fran O'Malley, worked with Bonnie Meszaros from the UD Center for Economic Education and Entrepreneurship to develop a course modeled on the Democracy Project for UD students preparing to become teachers. The course became a breadth requirement for all Elementary Teacher Education students, and since its inception in 2003, it has enrolled more than 2,500 students. Expanding on the vision of the Democracy Project, Freel initiated a winter session program in 2012 for UD undergraduates to study public affairs in Washington, DC. They learned from government leaders and served as interns for public and nonprofit agencies. After a few years under Freel's guidance, the program expanded in 2016 to an entire semester. Jointly offered with the Colin Powell School of Civic and Global Leadership at City College of New York, its chief instructor in 2019 was Mike Donilon, managing director of the Biden Institute, with Leann Moore from IPA providing operational support.[25] In 2019, IPA hosted the Delaware Summit on Civics Education, which focused on the need to develop a new vision for civics and civil discourse. "I think all Americans, regardless of ideology, can agree that the degrees of divisiveness, polarization, and incivility, coupled with increases in phenomena such as fake news, beg for improvements in the nature of civics education," said Fran O'Malley, director of The Democracy Project.[26]

The Biden School's commitment to promoting civic engagement and civil discourse was strengthened in May 2021, when the Stavros Niarchos Foundation (SNF) provided a grant for the Biden School to launch a new program called the SNF Ithaca Initiative. The initiative is designed to support innovative instruction in civic engagement and civil discourse for Biden School students and engage college students across the nation to

FIGURE 61. Joe Biden meets with the Washington Fellows
and program leaders Ed Freel and Mike Donilon, 2019.

FIGURE 62. Philip Barnes (PhD, UAPP 2015), faculty director, Stavros Niarchos Foundation Ithaca Initiative, teaching his class on civic discourse and democracy on the Green, September 21, 2021.

work in partnership to develop policy solutions to societal problems. The SNF Ithaca Initiative also sponsors new course offerings focused on civil discourse and funds graduate and undergraduate student scholarships, as well as providing support for the Biden Institute through subsidizing a series of new programs and special events, and sponsoring a bipartisan cohort of resident and visiting fellows. The Ithaca Initiative also supports Catherine McLaughlin in leading a national student dialogue on civic engagement and Valerie Biden Owens in offering a seminar series enabling students to hear from public servants across the political spectrum. Dean Aristigueta describes the overarching goal of the Ithaca Initiative as empowering "students with not just a firm grasp on their civic duties as citizens, but also their responsibilities within a diverse, multi-partisan civil society."[27]

The SNF funding supports a new endowed and named professorship in the Biden School, and a national search was launched to fill the position. While the search process was underway, Philip Barnes (PhD, UAPP 2015) was appointed faculty director of the initiative.[28] A professional staff member of the Institute for Public Administration and a faculty member in the Biden School, Barnes had already taught courses related to civil discourse and public policy. In the fall of 2021, he taught a course that focused entirely on this subject and was designed to become a foundational requirement for all undergraduates in the Biden School.[29] Barnes describes some of the prospects looking forward:

The Biden School now offers an entire 3-credit course that explores the intersection of public policy, civil discourse, and citizens in democratic societies. This course is just the beginning, and I expect there will be a sequence of courses, possibly building into a minor. Students in these courses will learn the critical skills of civil discourse—listening, perspective taking, building mutual respect, critical reasoning—and then practice and apply them to contemporary public policy deliberations. We are, in effect, training future public affairs professionals on how to navigate and operate in an increasingly diverse democracy. But we recognize that we cannot be content only to educate and train Biden School students and future public affairs professionals. The skills of civil discourse are needed across all realms of professional and civil life, meaning that we hope the Ithaca Initiative will extend across the entire university.[30]

The SNF Ithaca Initiative will enable civic engagement and civil discourse to become signature features of a Biden School education for both undergraduates and graduate students, and, in the longer term, signature features of a University of Delaware education.

FIGURE 63. Delaware Governor John Carney (MPA 1986) speaking at the Opportunity
Zone Summit sponsored with the Biden Institute, December 5, 2018.

CHAPTER NINE

LEGACIES AND POSSIBILITIES

THE SCHOOL OF PUBLIC POLICY AND ADMINISTRATION is "an exemplar of a new form of comprehensive public affairs school." That was the assessment of James L. Perry, Distinguished Professor Emeritus at the O'Neil School of Public and Environmental Affairs, Indiana University, nearly a decade before the Biden School was named and approved to be a freestanding professional school. Perry recognized that the University of Delaware's school was "on the cutting edge of integrating traditional scholarly research, education for professional leadership, and public service."[1] That assessment is more accurate now than ever before.

The history of the Biden School demonstrates that its emergence as a leading school of public affairs was by no means inevitable. At several critical junctures, the school might not have survived. The Division of Urban Affairs might not have continued after the Ford Foundation funding ended or after the change in university presidential leadership in 1968. The value of the College of Urban Affairs and Public Policy was challenged during another UD leadership transition in 1990, only to be reconfirmed for university support and defined as a model for other units. The school's future was also in doubt after the dissolution of the College of Human Services, Education and Public Policy in 2010. That challenge was also overcome, although the school went through a period of faculty contraction. Over its first sixty years, the school has operated under five different organizational arrangements and many different names. The Biden School has been a model of innovation, engagement, and resilience.

While the school's long-term future was never a foregone conclusion, school leaders and engaged faculty, staff, students, and alumni have always been committed to its mission and values and determined it would succeed. Together, they have demonstrated remarkable adaptability to the changing organizational forms of the school and the shifting expectations of university leaders. This adaptability is not surprising. The school was created to be an agent of organizational and social change. Particularly in its early decades, it attracted administrators, faculty, staff, and students who self-selected to be part of an innovative, change-oriented enterprise. Many possessed the knowledge, skills, and experience to be effective community and policy leaders.

Leadership responsibilities extended beyond the school's administrative heads to include center and program directors as well as faculty, staff, and students. Many were experienced in responding to fluid public policy environments and the emerging needs and demands of the communities they served, and that experience of working as change agents outside academia was an asset when changes to the school were required. Most of those who have worked in the school throughout its history, particularly those who have led it, never viewed it as a finished product.

Even with strong and inclusive internal leadership, the school would not have survived or prospered without the support of university leaders at various junctures. President John Perkins took the opportunity to launch an experimental interdisciplinary, action-oriented program, the Division of Urban Affairs. President E. Arthur Trabant transformed the non-academic division into a new graduate College of Urban Affairs and Public Policy. President David Roselle placed the school in a leadership position in the reorganization of five of the university's colleges into two. President Dennis Assanis recognized the potential of the Biden School and confirmed its priority in UD's development as a twenty-first-century engaged research university. The development of the Biden School over its first sixty years is thus a case study in higher educational leadership at both the university and program levels.

In some regards, the school's development has been a bellwether of the changing higher education landscape. It updated the nineteenth-century land-grant concept to address the needs and challenges of the late twentieth and early twenty-first centuries. The Biden School's dedication to interdisciplinary scholarship, its commitment to diversity as a dimension of quality, and its role in bridging the world of ideas and the world of action were ahead of their times.

DIFFERENT BY DESIGN

The Biden School was different by design. The Ford Foundation grant that led to the creation of the Division of Urban Affairs required that it be different from other academic units in its interdisciplinary identity and in the collaborations it supported between the university and the communities it served. When the division became the College of Urban Affairs and Public Policy, it was again designed to be different. It was one of only two graduate colleges in a predominantly undergraduate institution. Those two graduate colleges were given budgetary independence and responsibility far beyond that of any other academic unit.

The school's commitment to recruiting a graduate student body diverse in orientations and backgrounds was also built into its design. Candidates have been evaluated for admission based on professional experience and a commitment to using knowledge for social change as well as more traditional factors. Diversity has been an essential facet of the school's interdisciplinary approach and community focus. Beyond promoting racial diversity, the school's student composition has reflected increasing levels of gender diversity, with women outnumbering men among both undergraduate and graduate students. Notably, the school has also promoted geographic diversity, recruiting international students and promoting global research.

To carry out its mission, the Biden School has relied heavily on its centers and institutes, which have had a level of influence and independence not typical of most other academic units. That influence has been amplified because of the strength and continuity of the leadership of some of the centers. Leaders, as well as many faculty and staff, of the centers have sustained personal and institutional networks over time that have helped maintain these units' success in the face of changing economic conditions and shifting university priorities. The school has adopted policies and practices supporting the centers' and institutes' work and addressing their needs and priorities. This approach has had some unusual implications since the centers' and institutes' staffs and fiscal resources were at times greater than those of the school's academic programs, but the capacity of the centers and institutes has enabled the success of the *Delaware Model* of public affairs education.

The Biden School was also different from the mainstream of the university because it was designed to be engaged in applied research and service and to promote action based on the knowledge it created. The applied orientation of its programs and people has not always fit well with the prevailing academic structure or the embedded reward system that sustains that structure both at UD and across academia more broadly. Confronting this mismatch has been a continuing challenge for the school. After reflecting on the school's history, long-time faculty member Danilo Yanich concludes that "being different by design was a key to the school's success and also a key to its ongoing struggles."[2]

Because of its mission-based orientation, the Biden School has employed many non-tenure track faculty, most of whom were appointed to contribute to its applied research and public service mission. In some periods, the number of non-tenure track appointments has exceeded the number of tenure track faculty. Within the school's culture, the distinctions between tenure track and non-tenure track faculty have not been considered significant. The focus has been on what individuals contribute rather than on their titles or standing in the typical academic hierarchy. However, this has been at variance with the prevailing reward structure of the university. As a result, the differences in treatment between non-tenure track and tenure track faculty have remained an occasionally contentious issue of consequence for the university as a whole well into the twenty-first century.

Throughout its history, the school has grappled with how applied research and public service should be evaluated in promotion and tenure decisions. The school's approved criteria for these decisions has placed greater value on these activities than most other units. The school has also emphasized the importance of integrating teaching with research and public service. As a result, the Biden School has often needed to justify its decisions regarding faculty advancement and explain the importance of an integrated model of engaged scholarship to its identity as a professional and interdisciplinary school of public affairs.

The Biden School has employed many research and public service professionals, most of whom have worked in the centers and institutes and many of whom played vital roles in the overall development of the school, including its academic and research programs. While some have held secondary faculty appointments, most have not. When the Biden School became freestanding, it had more research and public service professionals than faculty. More than a dozen of these professionals had been serving in the school for decades. The professional staff have contributed exceptional expertise and experience in research, analysis, and public service delivery.[3] Supporting their success required targeted policies, such as the creation of a career ladder through which they could be promoted based on their research and public service accomplishments.

ADVANCING INQUIRY AND EDUCATION

The earliest iteration of the Biden School, the Division of Urban Affairs, was in the vanguard of interdisciplinary programs that created the field of urban affairs. Some of the division's faculty shaped the field through their scholarship and publications. The division also became the organizational hub for the Urban Affairs Association, which supported urban affairs programs across the country. Since the next iteration of the school, the College of Urban Affairs and Public Policy, had one of the first doctoral programs focused on urban affairs, its graduates created and led urban affairs programs at universities across the U.S. and beyond.

Some of the doctoral program's graduates were hired to join the faculty and professional staff of the school, a practice generally avoided in most traditional fields but one that made great sense for the development of the school's research, instructional, and public service programs. For example, John Byrne, Danilo Yanich, and Young-Doo Wang joined the school's faculty soon after completing their PhDs in 1980. Later in the school's development, other homegrown scholars joined the faculty and staff. As of July 2020, ten Biden School faculty members and twenty-one of its professional staff members had a doctoral or master's degree from the school.

For four decades, the focus of the school was exclusively on graduate education. Most of the graduate students were full-time and were supported through their work on the school centers' applied research and public service projects. The *Delaware Model* of public affairs education grew from this arrangement, enabling students to connect what they learned in their classes with how they could use that knowledge to improve communities and institutions. Years after he left the Biden School faculty, Robert Denhardt reflected on the impact of the *Delaware Model*: "What has been called *The Delaware Model* of combining classroom experiences with real-life engagement with public issues has set a high standard for public administration and public policy programs around the country. What's been done at Delaware is a more comprehensive integration of theory and practice in the student's experience than perhaps at any other school in the country."[4]

When the School of Urban Affairs and Public Policy developed undergraduate programs, it incorporated features of the *Delaware Model*. The undergraduate majors offered students educational opportunities parallel to those available to the school's graduate students.[5] However, the best representation of the integration of graduate and undergraduate education was in the development of 4+1 programs that enabled highly motivated and talented undergraduates to combine study under one of the school's undergraduate majors with the pursuit of one of its master's degrees in an accelerated program, providing students with opportunities typically only available to graduate students. Between 2015 and 2020, half of the university's Warner and Taylor award winners for the outstanding man and woman in the senior class were Biden School students.[6]

In an opinion article in *The News Journal* in 2012, Kristin Fretz and Neil Kirschling, two of the first graduates of the undergraduate Public Policy program, affirmed the value of an interdisciplinary public affairs education and their commitment to careers of public service: "The problems society faces are ever-changing and will affect all of us. They require an interdisciplinary approach and the combined engagement of all members of the community, especially those who will one day inherit these problems. If you dream of making a difference in the world, then you should act on that dream [and] together we can learn how to turn our dreams into careers that change the world."[7] The value of the Biden School's distinctive approach to public affairs education was also recognized by U.S. Senator Chris Coons, who proposed that what stands out about the school is "its interdisciplinary approach to learning with faculty committed to helping its students bridge the community of ideas and the community of action. Students are prepared to make a real difference in a wide range of areas including education, energy, budget, and healthcare."[8]

DELAWARE FIRST

Unquestionably, the most dramatic societal impact of the Biden School over its first sixty years has been in the state of Delaware. Indeed, this impact has been confirmed by external evaluation teams throughout the school's history. In 1961, when the Division of Urban Affairs was established, Delaware government agencies had little capacity for research, analysis, planning, and evaluation. Delaware state and local governments used virtually no data or policy analysis to inform decision-making, had no professional planning capabilities, and employed very few trained personnel in state or local service delivery. They also lacked officials with professional managerial experience to deal with the increasing demands for government services and the expansion of government agencies. For more than half a century, the Biden School's programs helped state and local governments and agencies develop these capabilities. In important respects, the governing capacity of the State of Delaware and the programs of the Biden School grew together, and in many areas became mutually dependent. That interdependence was greater than anything imagined when the Division of Urban Affairs was created.

One of the most important effects of the Biden School has been the professionalization of Delaware's public and nonprofit sectors. This began almost immediately after the Division of Urban Affairs was created, with its advocacy through the Greater Wilmington Development Council of hiring a professional planner for the City of Wilmington. Far beyond engaging in advocacy, however, the division developed programs that provided professional expertise: the Census and Data System, the Delaware Public Administration Institute, and the Urban Agent Division. These units offered government and community institutions professional policy, planning, program, and administrative services. While the initial focus of the division was on Wilmington, the scope quickly expanded across the state. All of its original programs expanded over the next half-century to become important units of the Biden School in 2021. New centers were added over the years in areas of emerging need in energy and environmental policy, historic preservation, and disaster science and management.

Early on in its development, the Biden School became the default research arm of Delaware's public policy decision-making system, ranging from providing projections of public school enrollments to evaluating the needs of senior citizens, from tracking the distribution of broadband capacity to studying the continuous improvement of transportation, energy, environmental, and social services. In a few cases, the Biden School has been officially designated as the agent of the State.[9]

Beyond providing enhanced research and professional services to local, county, and state government agencies, the Biden School's centers and institutes have also given direct technical assistance. For over half a century, many Delaware municipalities have relied upon the school's assistance to meet growing federal and state data and technical requirements and help develop proposals for federal and state funding. That assistance has most often been delivered by the Institute for Public Administration and the Center for Applied Demography and Survey Research. A similar pattern of assistance exists at the level of community development, particularly regarding neighborhood development in Wilmington. Those contributions began with the Urban Agent Program, expanded in the 1990s with the Wilmington Community Development Partnership, and continued through the first two decades of the twenty-first century through the Center for Community Research and Service's leadership of the Blueprint Communities program. All of these initiatives were focused on building community capacity for sustainable development, and all helped develop generations of community leaders and advocates.

In 2011, George C. Wright, Jr., the executive director of the Delaware League of Local Governments, explained that "eighty percent of Delaware's municipalities have populations under one thousand and have limited staff and resources. [We] consider IPA an essential partner in providing direct support and critical services to many of the state's local governments."[10] Wright's successor, Carl Luft, reflecting on that partnership, highlights IPA's role: "It's really hard to imagine how towns and cities in Delaware would address regulatory challenges and other issues . . . without IPA support. I don't know how they'd do it. Even some of the bigger municipalities have 'grown up' with IPA's assistance."[11] A similar sentiment has been expressed by James Baker, former mayor of Wilmington, who recognizes that faculty, staff, and students from the school "are an integral part of the Wilmington community and have been for decades" and have supported improved "services and community initiatives that have greatly benefitted our City's diverse population and neighborhoods."[12]

From its inception, the Division of Urban Affairs worked closely with the leadership of the Delaware business community, initially through collaborations with the Greater Wilmington Development Corporation. The alliance of business, government, and education leaders had a significant impact on creating the College of Human Services, Education and Public Policy. In the 2000s, the School of Public Policy and Administration worked closely with the Delaware State Chamber of Commerce and its associated think tank, the Delaware Public Policy Institute, to collaborate on health, education, and economic development issues. This collaboration led to further knowledge-based partnerships and a Knowledge-Based Partnership conference series used to leverage initiatives on crucial policy issues and launch new UD initiatives, including the Delaware Energy Institute, the Partnership for Public Education, and the Partnership for Healthy Communities.[13] Notably, all of these initiatives were university-wide, demonstrating the school's continuing role as a catalyst for UD innovation, especially in mobilizing the university's growing capacity for interdisciplinary, policy-oriented research. The contributions of the Biden School to Delaware over its first sixty years have been diverse and sustained.

MAKING A DIFFERENCE

Biden School alumni have become leaders across all sectors of the First State, most especially in state and municipal governments and in nonprofit and community institutions. At the time it became a freestanding professional school, those alumni included some of the state's most prominent elected leaders. John Carney was sworn in as governor of Delaware on January 17, 2017.[14] Lisa Blunt Rochester made history in 2016 when she was elected as Delaware's member of the House of Representatives, the first woman and first person of color to represent the state in Congress.[15] Michael Jackson (MPA, 1998) served as director of the Office of Management and Budget from 2017 to 2021, and Michael Morton (MPA, 1986) has been Delaware's Controller General since 2012. While both in office, they represented the chief budgetary officials for the executive and legislative branches of the state, and their staffs also included Biden School alumni. The same pattern holds with other state agencies. The school's Legislative Fellows program has provided the Delaware General Assembly with essential staff support. Many assembly members and leaders of state agencies are alumni,[16] and Delaware's county and local governments have also recruited a steady stream of Biden School graduates.

The Biden School has had a comparable impact on the Delaware nonprofit sector through its alumni, including those that graduated from its nonprofit management certificate program. Paul Calistro, an alumnus of the program and executive director of the West End Neighborhood House in Wilmington, indicates that he and other nonprofit leaders have made the program mandatory for their staff. The alumni of the school's degree programs and those who have participated in its professional development and certificate programs have formed a growing network of public and nonprofit professionals who have continued to work with the school long after graduation.[17]

Beyond the Biden School's contributions to the First State, its faculty and staff have cultivated extensive and growing national and global collaborations. At the national level, the school in its various iterations has worked with congressional offices, federal agencies, and institutes, such as the Centers for Disease Control and Prevention, and professional organizations such as the Network of Schools of Public Policy, Affairs and Administration, the American Society for Public Administration, the Association for Public Policy Analysis and Management, and the Urban Affairs Association. The research and analysis conducted by members of the school has influenced federal programs and practices in areas such as urban policy, energy and environmental policy, criminal justice, disaster science and management, and government administration.

The Biden School has also worked with diverse international organizations, including the Salzburg Global Seminar, the South African MISTRA think tank, the International Research Society for Public Management, and universities all over the world. In addition, the school faculty have participated in extensive global research collaborations on such issues as climate change, energy policy options, disaster mitigation and response, public sector leadership and administration, and historic preservation. Starting in the 1980s, the school attracted a steady stream of highly talented international students who returned to their countries after graduation and made their

FIGURE 64. U.S. Congressional Representative Lisa Blunt Rochester (MA, UAPP 2002) delivering the 2018 James R. Soles Lecture at UD, September 17, 2018.

marks in academic, government, and global nonprofit institutions. The school has sponsored Fulbright students, Muskie Fellows, and students from partner universities in Asia, Europe, Africa, and South and Central America.

POSSIBILITIES

The Biden School has enlarged and amplified the public purpose of the University of Delaware, acting as a catalyst for the development of UD as one of the nation's most engaged research universities. As a freestanding professional school, the Biden School now has the mandate to be an agent of change that will further enhance UD's overall impact on scholarship, education, and society.

Two facets of the school's historic mission will almost surely remain the same: the commitment to interdisciplinary inquiry on critical societal issues and the commitment to engaged scholarship that connects the world of ideas and the world of social action. At the start of the third decade of the twenty-first century, there is increasing recognition of the mismatch between the interdisciplinary knowledge required to address societal issues and the embedded disciplinary structure of universities. The prevailing organization of university faculty, a product of nineteenth- and twentieth-century development, is not aligned with the generation and dissemination of knowledge on some of the sociopolitical topics of greatest contemporary importance: energy, environment, urbanization, climate change, disaster mitigation, globalization, and the social determinants of health, education, and community development. The Biden School is organized not only to generate knowledge about such complex issues, but also to translate that knowledge into policies and programs.

The Biden School is organized to support UD's development as a research university. An underlying premise of all research universities is that investment in research serves a public purpose. Therefore, engaged scholarship is fundamental to the success of a twenty-first-century research university. In this regard, the Biden School will be an increasingly valuable asset for the University of Delaware. Engaged scholarship is built into the design of the school, and its continued development should strengthen UD's identity as one of the nation's leading engaged research universities.

In 1961, Joe Biden entered the University of Delaware as a freshman, becoming a Blue Hen. In the same year, UD launched the program that now bears his name. As Biden pursued a lifetime of public service, the school became a leader in public service education, preparing future generations to serve the constantly evolving needs of America and the wider world. The most enduring association between Joe Biden and the Biden School lies in shared values of civic engagement and public service. When Biden first met with the school's faculty shortly after the creation of the Biden Institute, he outlined areas of public policy for which the expertise of America's universities was needed: "civil rights, the justice system, the Constitution, violence

FIGURE 65. Joe Biden at the Biden is Back rally, April 7, 2017.

against women, environmental sustainability, and the access and affordability of higher education."[18] Beyond any specific policy needs, however, he focused on the necessity of promoting civic engagement in the democratic process and informed civil discourse on critical policy issues. In many regards, that was already the mission of the Biden School.

In 2021, the Biden School's mission statement was reaffirmed, reflecting values and priorities that had guided the school's development for sixty years:

Named for the 46th President of the United States, the Joseph R. Biden, Jr. School of Public Policy and Administration at the University of Delaware prepares students with the knowledge and skills necessary to engage in research and public service activities to improve the quality of life in communities around the world. Our faculty, staff, students, and alumni create and use interdisciplinary, non-partisan research and empirically-based analysis to inform effective decision-making and policy and to improve leadership and administration. We partner with organizations from all sectors to discover innovative and equitable solutions to the critical challenges of our time.[19]

In the long arc of history, President Joe Biden and UD will be inextricably interconnected. The University of Delaware will always be recognized as his alma mater. The school that bears his name will be the proud exemplar of that association.

NOTES

INTRODUCTION

1. Quoted in Peter Bothum, "New Name, Familiar Face," *UDaily*, December 11, 2018.
2. Daniel Rich and David Wilson, "White Paper: The Joseph R. Biden, Jr. School of Public Policy and Administration," unpublished, University of Delaware, June 17, 2016. Obtained from the author's collection of documents.
3. "The Biden School's Transition to a Free-Standing Professional School: A Report to the University Faculty Senate," February 10, 2020, 2. Courtesy of the Dean's Office, Biden School of Public Policy and Administration.
4. University of Delaware Graduate College enrollment report, October 2021. Courtesy of the Dean's Office, Biden School of Public Policy and Administration.
5. "Mission Statement," University of Delaware, accessed March 20, 2022, https://www.udel.edu/about/mission/
6. Stephen M. Gavazzi and E. Gordan Gee, *Land-Grant Universities for the Future: Higher Education for the Public Good* (Baltimore: Johns Hopkins University Press, 2018), 57.
7. G. Arno Loessner, "Ford Foundation Investment Is Delaware's Long-Term Gain: 50 Years of the School of Urban Affairs and Public Policy at the University of Delaware" (unpublished manuscript, 2012), 3. Courtesy of G. Arno Loessner.
8. Through the middle of the twentieth century, the primary public service program was the agricultural cooperative extension service.
9. The desegregation case revolved around whether the university was a state, and thereby public, entity subject to the most stringent interpretation of the Fourteenth Amendment. The university claimed it was not. In his ruling, Judge Seitz declared that it was.
10. Daniel Rich, "The Changing Political Economy of Higher Education: Public Investments and University Strategies," *South African Journal of Public Administration* 48, no. 3 (September 2013): 429–53.
11. J. R. Thelin, *A History of American Higher Education* (Baltimore: Johns Hopkins University Press, 2004), 260.
12. In the three decades after World War II, public university systems greatly expanded due to increased state funding for new campuses, academic programs, and university operations. The growth of state-level investments, combined with the incentives of the G.I. Bill, kept tuition rates low and drove an unprecedented increase in college enrollments. See ibid., 260–80.
13. John A. Munroe, *The University of Delaware: A History* (Newark: University of Delaware Press, 1986), 447.
14. Clark Kerr, *The Uses of the University* (Cambridge, MA: Harvard University Press, 1963), 52.

CHAPTER ONE: THE DIVISION OF URBAN AFFAIRS

1. Daniel Rich and Robert Warren, "The Intellectual Future of Urban Affairs: Theoretical, Normative and Organizational Options," *The Social Science Journal* 17, no. 2 (1980): 50–66.
2. John A. Perkins, "Proposal for an Urban Services Project for the University of Delaware," unpublished typescript, September 20, 1960, 2–5. Courtesy of the University of Delaware Archives and Records Management.
3. Ibid., 5–6.

4. The grant to UD was one of eight Ford Foundation urban affairs grants awarded across the nation.

5. Joseph McDaniel, Jr., Secretary of the Ford Foundation, to John A. Perkins, President of the University of Delaware, grant award letter, April 20, 1961. Courtesy of the University of Delaware Archives and Records Management.

6. Munroe, The *University of Delaware*, 385.

7. Overman served as director until 1968. He left UD to become the founding director of the Institute for Urban Studies at the University of Texas, Arlington.

8. Edward Overman, "The Division of Urban Affairs: First Two Years of Operation, July 1961–June 1963" (unpublished report, 1964), 1. Courtesy of UD Archives and Records Management.

9. George Worrilow had served as dean of the College of Agricultural Sciences and was familiar with the cooperative extension services that were part of the traditional land-grant mission.

10. G. Arno Loessner, "Ford Foundation Investment is Delaware's Long-Term Gain: 50 Years of the School of Urban Affairs and Public Policy at the University of Delaware" (unpublished typescript, 2012), 1. Courtesy of G. Arno Loessner.

11. Carol Hoffecker, *Corporate Capital: Wilmington in the Twentieth Century* (Philadelphia: Temple University Press, 1983).

12. Legendary for its philanthropy, the du Pont family was a generous benefactor to the University of Delaware. Most of the land on which the main campus is located was donated by Pierre S. du Pont and H. Rodney Sharp in 1915. The early endowment of the university grew from contributions by members of the family, and the university has continued to thrive from annual grants provided by the Unidel Foundation, set up from the estate of Amy du Pont solely to support the academic enrichment of the university. The names on many campus buildings bear witness to the du Pont legacy.

13. "Decennial Censuses, 1940–2010," U.S. Census Bureau, accessed May 5, 2019, http://www.census.gov/prod/www/decennial.html.

14. William W. Boyer served at the University of Delaware as Charles P. Messick Professor of Public Administration in the Department of Political Science. He later joined the Center for Applied Demography and Survey Research, developing a remarkably productive collaboration with the center's director, Edward Ratledge, that resulted in a series of books on Delaware policy and politics.

15. William W. Boyer, *Governing Delaware: Policy Problems in the First State* (Newark: University of Delaware Press, 2000), 94.

16. L. Ware, D. Rudder, and T. Davis, *The State of People of Color in Delaware: A Comparative Analysis of Racial Disparities in Income, Employment, Education, Homeownership, Business Ownership, and Involvement with the Criminal Justice System* (Wilmington, DE: Metropolitan Urban League, 2002).

17. C. H. Brown and K. O'Connor, "Population Analysis of Wilmington and New Castle County" (Working Paper Number 4) (Newark: Division of Urban Affairs, University of Delaware, 1963). Retrieved from UD Archives and Records Management.

18. Jason Bourke, "Urban Governance and Economic Development: An Analysis of the Changing Political Economy of Wilmington, Delaware, 1945–2017" (PhD diss., University of Delaware, 2018). Jason Bourke received his PhD from the Biden School in 2018. His dissertation chronicles the changes in Wilmington's political economy and economic revitalization efforts over the seventy years following World War II.

19. Timothy K. Barnekov and Daniel Rich, "Business and Urban Development" (unpublished typescript, 1975). From the author's collection of documents.

20. Timothy K. Barnekov and Daniel Rich, "Privatism and Urban Development: An

Analysis of the Organized Influence of Local Business Elites," *Urban Affairs Quarterly* 12, no. 4 (1977): 431–60.

21. The division staff convinced the GWDC to broaden its initial focus on the Wilmington central business district and consider the changing regional economy.

22. Overman, "Division," 8.

23. Ibid., 13.

24. Joe Biden, *Promises To Keep: On Life And Politics* (New York: Random House, 2007), 4.

25. Ibid., 46.

26. Hoffecker, *Corporate*, 206.

27. Ibid., 207. The hospital decision confirmed in 1975 also favored the suburbs. The new hospital would be in the center of New Castle County, reflecting the new locus of population and development.

28. Federal Judge Murray Schwartz had declared the unitary principle as the foundation of his decision, anticipating that all Northern New Castle County residents needed to be in the same school district to ensure that all students would be treated equitably.

29. Jeffrey Raffel, a professor appointed in 1971 and later director of the school, published the seminal work on the process. Jeffrey A. Raffel, *The Politics of School Desegregation: The Metropolitan Remedy in Delaware* (Philadelphia: Temple University Press, 1980).

30. Overman, "Division," 9.

31. Ibid.

32. Edward Ratledge graduated from UD in 1972 with a BS and MA in Economics before joining the division.

33. Edward Ratledge, email message to author, July 17, 2019.

34. Ibid.

35. Overman, "Division," 7.

36. G. Arno Loessner began his UD career in November 1969 in the Division of Urban Affairs. In 1978, he was appointed the executive assistant to the university president and university secretary, and in 1986, he also was appointed vice president for advancement. In 2012, he became the first chair of the Biden School's Board of Advisors.

37. Loessner, "Ford," 1–2.

38. Jeffrey Raffel, email message to author, May 20, 2019.

39. These efforts eventually led to the creation of the Delaware Community Reinvestment Action Council (DECRAC) in 1987, an organization devoted to supporting the implementation of the federal Community Reinvestment Act of 1977.

40. Jerome Lewis joined UD in 1969 after completing his PhD in Public Administration at New York University. In addition to leading the Institute for Public Administration for half a century, he worked with William Boyer to establish the MPA program. He became one of the key advocates for what would become the *Delaware Model* of public affairs education.

41. These functions continue in the Biden School as of 2021.

42. Loessner, "Ford," 2.

43. Raffel, email message to author, May 20, 2019.

44. Robert Wilson, email message to author, July 24, 2019.

45. Raffel, email message to author, May 20, 2019.

46. William C. Pendleton, *Urban Studies and the University—The Ford Foundation Experience* (New York: Ford Foundation Reprints, 1974), 5.

CHAPTER TWO: THE COLLEGE OF URBAN AFFAIRS AND PUBLIC POLICY

1. Mary Helen Callahan helped launch the Council of University Institutes of Urban Affairs (1975–80) and then served as executive director of the Urban Affairs Association

(UAA) from 1980 to 2000. For thirty years, she also served as a special assistant to the dean of the College (and then School) of Urban Affairs and Public Policy and the college's chief communications professional. Margaret Wilder, who had been a faculty member in the Biden School and became the executive director of UAA, describes Callahan as a transformative leader responsible for "the sustainability of a multi-disciplinary organization, and the core reasons for UAA's continued relevance." Email message to author, October 13, 2021.

2. Daniel Rich and Robert Warren, "The Intellectual Future of Urban Affairs: Theoretical, Normative and Organizational Options," *The Social Science Journal* 17/2 (1980): 50–66.

3. Munroe, *The University of Delaware*, 409.

4. Ibid., 385.

5. Creating a law school had been considered by the Board of Trustees but was rejected because of the expected cost of launching a high-quality program.

6. "A Community Design: Division of Urban Affairs," in *The Decade Ahead: The Report of the Community Design Planning Commission*, vol. 2 (unpublished, University of Delaware, 1971), 5. Courtesy of UD Archives and Records Management.

7. The College of Marine Studies represented UD's designation as a federally funded sea-grant university, responsible for a broad range of programs supporting research and education to improve the conservation of coastal and marine resources.

8. David Ames became the cofounder of the Center for Historic Architecture and Engineering (later Design) with Bernard Herman in 1984, which he then directed for thirty years. Ames also was instrumental in establishing the original concentration in preservation as part of the MA in Urban Affairs and Public Policy.

9. David Ames, email message to author, June 18, 2019. In 1971, new faculty were hired with primary appointments in the Division of Urban Affairs (Mark Haskell, Jeffrey Raffel, and James H. Sills). Some senior staff members were awarded faculty rank in the division (C. Harold Brown, Francis Tannian, and Robert Wilson).

10. Ibid.

11. Ibid.

12. Some of the nation's leading social science scholars engaged in a battle that often entangled university departments and national and international academic and professional communities. Each discipline had a set of active protagonists who had large numbers of disciples: in sociology, Talcott Parsons and C. Wright Mills; in political science, David Easton and Sheldon Wolin; in economics, Milton Friedman and G.L.S. Shackle.

13. Irving Louis Horowitz, "Big Five and Little Five: Measuring Revolutions in Social Science," *Society* (March/April 2006): 9–12. Horowitz noted other new fields including environmental studies, criminology, and communications.

14. Danilo Yanich, email message to author, June 8, 2020.

15. Jeffrey Raffel, email message to author, May 20, 2019

16. Francis Tannian, email message to author, July 8, 2019.

17. Robert Wilson, email message to author, July 24, 2019.

18. Quoted in the University of Delaware *Messenger* 15, No. 1 (2007).

19. Given that the PhD in Urban Affairs and Public Policy was one of the nation's leading programs in a new field, the college hired some of its doctoral graduates. John Byrne (1980), Young-Doo Wang (1980), and Danilo Yanich (1980) all had long and productive careers on the faculty. The college also hired master's and doctoral graduates as research and public service professional staff in the centers. Some of the senior professional staff also held faculty rank.

20. David Ames, email message to author, November 10, 2019.

21. The external review team visit was part of the Faculty Senate's Academic Program Review (APR) process for the periodic evaluation of all academic programs. The recommendations from the APR external review team were summarized in the College of Urban Affairs and Public Policy *Annual Report for 1987–88* (unpublished, 1988), 4. From the author's collection of documents. Unless otherwise indicated, unpublished documents cited in this chapter were similarly obtained from the author's collection. Concurrent with the APR, a 1987 report of the National Association of State Universities and Land-Grant Colleges (now the Association of Public and Land-Grant Universities) cited the college as "a model" because of the breadth of its research and engagement across a wide range of issues, noting that it was "responsive to both external clients . . . and to internal disciplinary concerns." Quoted in Callahan, "A Brief History of the College of Urban Affairs and Public Policy (unpublished, University of Delaware, 1996), 3.

22. The Messick Chair was established in honor of Charles P. Messick, a 1907 graduate of the university who, for more than forty years, devoted his talents to addressing the problems of governmental administration in the state of New Jersey and the nation.

23. William W. Boyer, email message to author, March 11, 2019.

24. Ibid.

25. In 1988, the UD MPA program was granted permission to establish a chapter of Pi Alpha Pi, the national honor society for programs in public affairs and administration.

26. College of Urban Affairs and Public Policy, *Annual Report for 1989–90* (unpublished, 1990).

27. Ibid.

28. Center for Historic Architecture and Design, "CHAD: Halfway to Historic, 1984–2009" (unpublished, University of Delaware, 2010), 3. Courtesy of Chandra Reedy.

29. Chandra Reedy joined UD in 1989 after completing her PhD in Archeology at UCLA. In addition to her faculty appointment in the Biden School, she held a joint appointment in Art History. Her research focuses on the preservation of traditional technologies and their associated materials and intangible cultural heritage. She directed the Center for Historic Architecture and Design's Laboratory for the Analysis of Cultural Materials, and much of her fieldwork was done in Asia.

30. Chandra Reedy, email message to author, May 24, 2019.

31. Ibid.

32. Ibid.

33. Mary Helen Callahan, "Brief History."

34. A separate MA in Historic Preservation was initiated much later but was not sustained. The concentration in the MA program continued to be supported by the center.

35. CHAE also received funding from the National Endowment for the Humanities to develop, from the Federal Direct Tax of 1789, a reconstruction of early republican era landscape to improve historical preservation policies in Delaware. Callahan, "Brief History."

36. In the 1980s and 1990s, Warren supervised more doctoral dissertations than any other faculty member, and some of his students later became leaders of urban affairs programs at other universities.

37. James G. Strathman, "A Ranking of US Graduate Programs in Urban Studies and Urban Affairs," *Journal of Urban Affairs* 14, no. 1 (1992): 79–92.

38. College of Urban Affairs and Public Policy, *Annual Report for 1989–90*.

39. Graham Hall originally had been an elementary school. After the New Castle County district consolidation to achieve desegregation in 1974, and subsequent restructuring in 1981, the newly created Christina School District no longer needed the building. A state law enabled the expedited transfer of surplus public school facilities to other public education institutions. As a result, the building was transferred to the university for a nominal fee.

40. Barnekov later served as acting dean of the college and then director of the Center for Community Development. As described in Chapter 5, Barnekov became dean of the College of Human Resources, Education and Public Policy in 2001.

41. The professional staff focused on research and applied research. The support staff maintained operating systems and services (such as the survey research center, which is a part of CADSR) and provided administrative assistance.

42. Ibid.

43. Munroe, *The University of Delaware*, 411, 447.

44. Roselle had been president of the University of Kentucky. He previously served as provost at Virginia Tech. A mathematician, he had earlier been Virginia Tech's dean of research and graduate studies.

45. See Strathman, "Ranking." In addition to ranking fourth overall, Delaware was ranked #1 by peer institution leaders. The ranking was based on a combination of peer evaluations and citations of the faculty's published work.

46. In 2018, Schneider received the UD College of Arts and Sciences Distinguished Alumni Award.

47. College of Urban Affairs and Public Policy, *Annual Report for 1991–92* (unpublished, University of Delaware, 1992), 2. The Review Committee report affirmed that the college "has gained the respect and good will of local, state and regional officials and national colleagues in the field of urban affairs and public policy." The committee also noted that "the college is underappreciated in the university where its image is not as strong as it is regionally, nationally and internationally."

48. The concentration in historic preservation and planning was partly a compromise response to external pressure to prepare American Planning Association-certified planners for local governments. The college did not have the faculty capacity to support a new planning degree. However, the concentration would produce graduates with sufficient planning expertise to be employed by local governments for entry-level positions. The graduates would have the added advantage of understanding historic preservation planning, a specialty that most local governments did not have the resources to support as a separate position.

49. Gift funds also increased, enabling the development of small endowments, including scholarship funds.

50. Of particular importance, the college and the university administration came to a formal agreement on the terms governing the college's budgeting system. The agreement confirmed the college's high level of independence along with its responsibilities for generating a growing level of operating support from external sources and systematically reporting its budget status.

CHAPTER THREE: POLICY PARTNERSHIPS AND THE *DELAWARE MODEL*

1. College of Urban Affairs and Public Policy, *Annual Report for 1990–91* (unpublished, University of Delaware, 1991). Courtesy of UD Archives and Records Management.

2. Mary Helen Callahan, "Urban Affairs and Public Policy Newsletter" (Spring 1993): 6.

3. Daniel Rich, "Report to the Provost" (unpublished, University of Delaware, 1995), 6. From the author's collection of documents.

4. Sponsored research and public service per full-time equivalent (FTE) college faculty increased to over $300,000 in 1995, among the highest level of any academic unit at the university, including the science and engineering departments.

5. Rich, "Report," 6.

6. Quoted in Callahan, "Brief History," 6.

7. Ibid., 9.

8. Ibid.

9. The first study of homelessness in Delaware was conducted by Steven Peuquet, a city planner and urban economist, who joined the Urban Agent Division in 1983 and became director of the Center for Community Development, which evolved from that division, in 2005.

10. Callahan, "Urban Affairs" (1993), 13.

11. Before joining the university, Sills had, in 1963, become the first Black executive director of Peoples Settlement in Wilmington. He was an early and strong advocate for neighborhood improvement through community development organizations and for removing political and economic barriers facing Blacks.

12. Mary Helen Callahan, "Urban Affairs and Public Policy Newsletter" (Spring 1994): 6.

13. The Urban Agent Program was renamed the Urban Agent Division in 1976.

14. He became director again in 2005, serving until his retirement in 2018.

15. In 1993, CCD, the Delaware State Housing Authority, and the Delaware Community Foundation formed the Housing Capacity-Building Program, providing grants to non-profit organizations to expand their housing assistance programs. CCD also worked with the City of Wilmington and New Castle County to develop Comprehensive Housing Affordability Strategies to qualify each jurisdiction for financial assistance across various federal programs.

16. Quoted in Callahan, "Urban Affairs" (1994), 12. Gilman retired from the college in 1992 and served as professor emeritus until he died in 1998.

17. Ibid., 2.

18. Loessner led nearly two dozen graduate study abroad programs over four decades.

19. As UD vice president and secretary, Loessner took the lead in promoting the partnership with the Salzburg Seminar.

20. Timothy Barnekov, Barry Cullingworth, Dan Rich, Paul Solano, and Robert Warren were visiting scholars at the University of Strathclyde in the 1980s. The college hosted a half-dozen visiting scholars from among the Strathclyde faculty.

21. The results included two books by Cullingworth, one updating earlier work on planning in the U.K. and another on planning in the U.S., a series of articles, and a jointly authored book: Timothy K. Barnekov, Robin Boyle, and Daniel Rich, *Privatism and Urban Policy in Britain and the United States* (New York: Oxford University Press, 1989). Rich continued as a visiting professor at Strathclyde through 2004.

22. IPA staff also undertook a project, with the assistance of the Salzburg Seminar and the Hewlett Foundation, to extend the concept and function of IPA to universities in the former Soviet Union. This led to a key partnership with Babes-Bolyai University in Romania.

23. Since the 1970s, the center had worked with the UD Institute for Energy Conversion, the federal government's designated center of excellence for research on photovoltaics. That collaboration focused on policies related to photovoltaics and other solar energy options. This association became a growing partnership between faculty and students in science and engineering and those in the policy sciences. In 1994, the center received funding from the U.S. National Renewable Energy Laboratory to examine the economic and environmental dimensions and policy implications of photovoltaics as a demand-side management tool.

24. The center's study was a new initiative by the World Bank under its "Alternative Energy Paths" project.

25. Quoted in Callahan, "Urban Affairs" (1994), 2.

26. John Byrne was a contributing author to the Second and Third Assessment Reports of the Intergovernmental Panel on Climate Change.

27. Initially, the book series was published by Transaction Books, and later published by Routledge.

28. The program's name was subsequently switched to Energy and Environmental Policy, parallel to the center's name. While the program was sponsored by CEEP, UD policy precluded centers from administering degree programs. The issue of a suitable administrative home for cross-college interdisciplinary programs was not resolved until UD created the Graduate College in 2019.

29. Robert Denhardt, Jerome R. Lewis, Jeffrey A. Raffel, and Daniel Rich, "Integrating Theory and Practice in MPA Education: The Delaware Model," *Journal of Public Administration Education* 3, no. 2 (1997): 153–62.

30. Ibid., 152–53.

31. Ibid., 155.

32. Institute for Public Administration, "Legislative Fellows Program Update" (unpublished, University of Delaware, 2019), 3. Courtesy of the Institute for Public Administration.

33. IPA Program Manager Lisa Moreland Allred pointed out that the "kind of research and staffing of standing committees that our fellows are involved in is usually done by full-time professionals in other states" (Ibid., 5).

34. As of 2019, 315 graduate and undergraduate students had served as fellows (ibid.).

35. Quoted in *School of Public Policy and Administration: 50 Years* (Newark: University of Delaware Office of Communications and Marketing, 2012), 11.

36. Ibid., 9.

CHAPTER FOUR: THE SCHOOL OF URBAN AFFAIRS AND PUBLIC POLICY

1. Schiavelli became provost in July 1994. He was an experienced academic leader, having served as provost and interim president at the College of William and Mary.

2. In support of consolidating the colleges of Education, Human Resources, and Urban Affairs and Public Policy, the deans' advisory letter proposed that these units were "linked by the common mission of being interdisciplinary pre-professional and professional programs with a policy and service orientation directed to central societal issues and challenges." The programs were complimentary and were connected by "an historic association with the university's responsibilities as a state-assisted, land grant institution and share a commitment to academic and professional values that emphasize interdisciplinary research and instruction in the service of meeting important societal needs." UD Deans to Provost Melvyn Schiavelli, "Advisory Letter on College Reorganization," October 17, 1995, 2. From the author's collection of documents. Unless otherwise noted, other primary documents cited are from the author's collection.

3. The academic units were the School of Urban Affairs and Public Policy, two academic departments focused on public education that later joined to become the School of Education, the Department of Individual and Family Studies, the Department of Consumer Economics and Apparel Design, and the Department of Hotel, Restaurant and Institutional Management.

4. When Barnekov became dean, Pamela Leland became acting director of the Center

for Community Development and Family Policy. In 2002, the center's name was changed to the Center for Community Research and Service, and Leslie Cooksey was appointed director. The center continued to offer programs to address issues faced by lower-income communities in Delaware and strengthen the capacity of nonprofit organizations. In 2004, Steve Peuquet was appointed director.

5. Daniel Rich, "The College of Human Services, Education and Public Policy: A Progress Report" (unpublished typescript, 2000).

6. Ibid., 1.

7. The *Engaged University* model aimed at making the campus a more vital part of the fabric of its community. Engagement was viewed as a two-way process for defining needs and priorities and exchanging ideas and resources: "Embedded in the engagement ideal is a commitment to sharing and reciprocity. By engagement the Commission envisioned partnerships, two-way streets defined by mutual respect among the partners for what each brings to the table." J. Byrne, *Public Higher Education Reform Five Years After the Kellogg Commission on the Future of State and Land-Grant Universities* (Washington, DC: National Association of State Universities and Land-Grant Colleges, 2006), 7.

8. Kellogg Commission on the Future of State and Land-Grant Universities (Kellogg Commission), *Returning to Our Roots: The Engaged Institution* (Washington, DC: National Association of State Universities and Land-Grant Colleges, 1999), 46.

9. Ibid.

10. The funding for CHEP line items was especially significant since the state's allocations for support of general UD operations were not keeping up with the rise in overall costs.

11. Secondary teacher education programs were in the College of Arts and Sciences. Most UD colleges had programs that provided services for K–12 public education, such as the economic education program in the Lerner College of Business and Economics.

12. The Center for Disabilities Studies was established under the UD Research Office and transferred to CHEP.

13. These partnerships included the New Castle County Professional Development Council (with the superintendents of five New Castle County school districts); the Delaware Academy of School Leadership partnership (with the Business/Public Education Council and the Department of Education); the Milford Professional Development School (with the Milford School District and the State of Delaware); the Institute for Public Administration's partnership with the Delaware Public Policy Institute; and ongoing programs connecting the work of CHEP centers to the Governor's Family Services Cabinet Council.

14. Functionally, the situation was more complex since many of those working in the centers, particularly the professional staff, also felt allegiance to the school even though they didn't have academic appointments.

15. Jeffrey A. Raffel, "Founding the School of Urban Affairs and Public Policy" (unpublished, March 11, 2019), 3. Courtesy of Jeffrey A. Raffel. Raffel's recollections, initially shared in draft documents to the author, have been published in his memoir *Lessons Learned: A Memoir of Leadership Development* (Washington, DC: NASPAA, 2019).

16. The center directors insisted on retaining control of graduate student funding decisions. At the same time, the school had limited graduate student funding options apart from the centers. Most of the external funding came through the centers, and since the school had no undergraduate programs, it had no teaching assistantships.

17. The policy was adopted because many federal sponsors were not providing tuition support in contracts and grants. In addition, the provision of matching graduate tuition support would provide an incentive to increase external funding and graduate student stipend support.

18. Raffel, "Founding," 5.

19. Ibid. While most of the funding was from external sources, the total number of awards included some competitive university fellowships and minority graduate scholarships.

20. Callahan, "Urban Affairs" (1993), 1. Courtesy of UD Archives and Records Management.

21. Ibid.

22. Ibid.

23. Jeffrey Raffel, email message to author, May 20, 2019.

24. Quoted in College of Arts and Sciences, "School of Urban Affairs and Public Policy: Integrating Academic Excellence and Professional Experience" (unpublished, University of Delaware, 2012), 9.

25. Timothy K. Barnekov, email message to author, June 27, 2019. Barnekov reports that sometimes this meant that non-tenure track faculty had to do two jobs—one being the support of the externally and contract-funded work of the centers and the other being the teaching, academic supervision, and publishing associated with tenure track faculty.

26. Ibid. Barnekov reports that the expectation of increased external funding was rarely fulfilled. Tenure track faculty in these appointments, especially junior faculty, focused on generating publications to support promotion and tenure. Typically, they were uninterested in the project work of the centers or in generating external funds for their work.

27. Raffel, "Lessons Learned," 83.

28. Quoted in the UD *Messenger* 13 (November 3, 2005). Stein was chair of the Department of Consumer Studies until the move of the Leadership program. She became program director of the undergraduate Leadership program in the school in 2005 and remained director through 2021.

29. Raffel, "Lessons Learned," 88.

30. NASPAA later kept the acronym but changed its name to the Network of Schools of Public Policy, Affairs and Administration, intended to denote a larger global scope. Raffel chaired the committee that recommended the name change.

31. Two faculty received prestigious NASPAA awards—Jerome Lewis received the Elmer B. Staats Public Service Award (1998) and Eric Jacobson (MPA 1981) received the Leslie A. Whittington Excellence in Teaching Award (2004).

32. The urban-grant designation was later dropped by the federal government.

33. Daniel Rich, "The University of Delaware as an Engaged University," presentation to the Consortium of University Public Service Organizations, Newark, Delaware, March 15, 2006.

34. Although the overall level of state funding was relatively flat during the Roselle administration, CHEP and the new College of Health Sciences generated targeted support from the state that would otherwise not have been forthcoming.

CHAPTER FIVE: THE SCHOOL OF PUBLIC POLICY AND ADMINISTRATION

1. Harker spent his entire academic career at the University of Pennsylvania, starting as an undergraduate, completing his doctoral degree in civic and environmental engineering, and rising to become the youngest faculty member to be awarded an endowed professorship in Wharton's history. Prior to being appointed Wharton School dean in 2000, Harker was interim dean and deputy dean, as well as the chair of its operations and information management department.

2. As the DuPont company's presence in Delaware contracted, the state's role as the back-office credit card capital for the banking industry grew, resulting in partnerships between the university and leaders from that sector, initially MBNA.

3. George Irvine, "Whither Publicness? The Changing Public Identities of Research Universities" (PhD Diss., University of Delaware, 2018), 260.

4. AAU's sixty-two research universities (thirty-six public/twenty-six private) earn the majority of the competitively awarded federal funding for research and are recognized as the "elite" among the nation's institutions offering graduate and professional education. Membership is by invitation. Earning an invitation means demonstrating that the research and education profile of the university exceeds the median of current member institutions.

5. A premium was on the federal funding that qualified in the AAU membership requirements.

6. The Health Sciences Alliance was a partnership between UD, Thomas Jefferson University in Philadelphia (which had a medical school with designated seats for Delawareans funded by the state), the Nemours Foundation (which supported a renowned hospital for children), and Christiana Care (Delaware's largest health provider). The new research institutes, UDEI and DENIN, were designed to generate the capacity to compete for larger research grants.

7. Center for Budget and Policy Priorities, "Recent Deep State Higher Education Cuts May Harm Students and the Economy for Years to Come" (2013). Retrieved from http://www.cbpp.org/cms/?fa=view&id=3927.

8. American Association for the Advancement of Science (AAAS), "Historical Trends in Federal R&D" (2016). Retrieved from http://www.aaas.org/page/historical-trends -federal-rd.

9. Irvine, "Whither," 294. By 2015, UD research obligations were slightly below their level in 2005, under $80 million. UD had a 33 percent decrease in federal research obligations between 2010 and 2015, a pattern similar to that of other research universities but more severe than most.

10. Ibid., 265. Irvine concluded that UD remained affordable and accessible to those families above the median household income mark. However, for those below the median, UD became increasingly less accessible unless they received tuition assistance of some kind.

11. F. Berry, "The Changing Climate for Public Affairs Education," NASPAA presidential address, Washington, DC, October 1, 2010.

12. Ibid.

13. Public service faculty were non-tenure track (renamed continuing track) faculty. They were funded in part from state allocations to focus a significant portion of their workload on public service programs, applied research, and technical assistance to the state and its communities.

14. A CHEP priority was the reconfiguration of space and facilities so that most of the academic units would be in proximity to each other.

15. Initiatives to develop joint programs failed, including a proposal for a doctoral-level leadership program to build upon and expand the Doctor of Education (EdD) program. The new degree program would combine the expertise of the School of Education faculty and the MPA faculty in the school with some contributions from other CHEP units. The proposed program would fill a gap at UD since there was no professionally oriented doctoral program in business administration or public administration. The new program was expected to attract senior professionals from all sectors and generate additional graduate tuition revenue.

16. Jeffrey A. Raffel, "Founding," 3.

17. Apple earned his doctorate in physical chemistry at UD in 1982. In 1991, he joined the faculty of Rensselaer Polytechnic Institute and served as chemistry department chair from 1997 until 2001. He became dean of graduate education in 2001 and vice provost in 2002. Apple joined UD in July 2005 as dean of the College of Arts and Sciences and professor of chemistry.

18. At a Faculty Senate-sponsored hearing, many school faculty expressed concern that independent status would not be supported by the administration.

19. Maria Aristigueta started her career as an evaluator for the U.S. Accounting Office and served as a senior management analyst for the Florida cities of Orlando and Miami. She joined the UD faculty in 1997 after receiving her doctorate from the University of Southern California and teaching at the University of Central Florida.

20. This included the Institute for Public Administration, Center for Community Research and Service, Center for Applied Demography and Survey Research, and Center for Historic Architecture and Design.

21. In three years, CEEP and ENEP moved to the College of Arts and Sciences, with the ENEP program rejoining the school.

22. Quoted in Dan Rich, "The School of Public Policy and Administration Celebrates 50 Years," *CONNECT* 4, no. 1 (2012), 3.

23. Quoted in *School of Public Policy and Administration: 50 Years* (Newark: University of Delaware Office of Communications and Marketing, 2012), 11.

24. Between 2014 and 2016, they switched roles, enabling Aristigueta to serve as president of the American Society of Public Administration.

25. The members of the initial Board of Advisors were Tony Allen (PhD, UAPP 2001), Bank of America communications executive and UD Trustee; Raina Harper Allen (MA, UAPP 2001), Director, Community Engagement and Programs to Lieutenant Governor Matt Denn; Kenneth Becker (MA, UAPP 1976), president of Becker Capital and finance and managing partner, EcogySolar; Walter Broadnax, SPPA Messick Fellow and distinguished professor, The Maxwell School, Syracuse University; The Hon. Jeffrey W. Bullock, Delaware Secretary of State; Robert Denhardt, Charles P. Messick Professor Emeritus, and former dean and professor, Arizona State University; Kim Gomes (MPA 2004), vice president, The Byrd Group; G. Arno Loessner, UD professor emeritus (chair); Renosi Mokate (MA, UAPP 1983 and PhD, UAPP 1986), executive director (Angola, Nigeria, and South Africa) of the World Bank Group; Paul Posner, professor of public administration, George Mason University, and former president of ASPA; John H. Taylor, Jr., senior vice president and executive director, Delaware Public Policy Institute; Sibusiso Vil-Nkomo (MA, UAPP 1983 and PhD, UAPP 1995), 2011–12 J. William Fulbright Research Scholar at Fordham University and research professor at the University of Pretoria; and Jane Vincent (MPA 1995), U.S. Housing and Urban Development regional administrator for the mid-Atlantic.

26. The Delaware Public Policy Institute and the Institute for Public Administration cosponsored conferences focused on key state and national policy issues.

27. Pierce joined the school faculty in 2011 after having worked on public policy issues at the Brookings Institution and with the White House Council on Environmental Policy.

28. In 2014, the school had 252 undergraduate majors (149 in OCL and 103 in PP) and 290 minors (108 in OCL, 33 in PP, and 149 in PH).

29. School of Urban Affairs and Public Policy, "Academic Program Review Self-Study," (unpublished, University of Delaware, April 2014), 24. From the author's collection of documents.

30. A former Delaware Secretary of State, Freel was a senior advisor to U.S. Senator Thomas Carper. The Washington Fellows program became a full-semester option in the spring of 2016.

31. The DISA program was approved by the Faculty Senate in April 2009 and obtained seed funding from a $400,000 grant from the Unidel Foundation. The first students entered the program in the fall of 2010. The program was given permanent status in 2016.

32. DRC support came from the National Science Foundation, the Department of Homeland Security, and the U.S. Department of Health and Human Services. Other funding sources have included the NOAA Sea Grant Program, Federal Emergency Management Agency, Multidisciplinary Center for Earthquake Engineering Research, Public Entity Risk Institute, and U.S. Geological Survey.

33. From 2009 to 2014, the school's faculty maintained a very high level of scholarly productivity that included publishing 121 refereed journal articles, seventeen books, forty-two book chapters, and dozens of technical reports, book reviews, conference papers, and proceedings.

34. SUAPP, "Academic Program Review Self-Study," 77.

35. Princeton had among the most expensive programs in the nation but was discounting its graduate tuition rate by 90 percent.

36. As of 2013–14, the cost of the UD MPA was $63,546, higher than all national competitors, public or private.

37. The program provided a 50 percent graduate tuition scholarship for Delawareans, a 35 percent scholarship for U.S. nationals, and a 10 percent scholarship for international students.

38. The additional challenge for the school's MPA program (and, to a lesser extent, other master's level programs) is that the university is not located in a large urban area enabling it to draw significant numbers of part-time applicants. As a result, the MPA program was designed for full-time students, who must pay full tuition. The basis for the *Delaware Model* was having such full-time students who could devote significant time to public service projects, as well as classes and applied research.

39. As a faculty member and chair of the Department of Political Science and International Relations, Pika had developed many close connections with colleagues in the school.

40. Ralph J. Begleiter, "The Joseph R. and Jill T. Biden Delaware Institute Project Summary, Status and Analysis: A Report for the College of Arts and Sciences and the University of Delaware" (Center for Political Communication, University of Delaware, 2016), 3.

41. Ralph Begleiter, email message to author, March 25, 2020.

42. Begleiter, "Project Summary," appendix, 1.

43. Begleiter reports no actual engagement with Biden on his senatorial papers until much later. Negotiations between UD and Biden's attorney over his papers began in early 2011, and the formal agreement was signed in late 2011 (email message to author, June 15, 2020).

44. Ibid.

45. Ralph Begleiter, email message to author, June 28, 2020.

46. Plouffe and Schmidt did not receive their UD degrees until 2010 and 2013, respectively.

47. Cited in Begleiter, "Project Summary," 5.

48. Ralph Begleiter, email message to author, March 25, 2020.

49. The Center for Political Communication adopted the phrase "epicenter of politics" as its catch line (Begleiter, "Project Summary," 5).

50. This change in designation happened because, at UD, "Institute" is the designation that has been used for a university-wide unit, while "Center" is used for a college unit.

51. Biden Papers Gift Agreement, 2011, cited in Begleiter, "Project Summary," 13.

52. A college-based team that included Pika, Begleiter, and CAS Dean Watson examined social science buildings at other universities as potential models.

53. Ralph Begleiter, email message to author, June 15, 2020.

54. Joseph Pika, email message to author, June 16, 2020.

55. Joseph Pika, email message to author, March 25, 2020.

56. Quoted in Ann Mansur, "Vice President Biden Speaks, Donates Papers," *UDaily*, September 16, 2011.

57. Ibid.

58. Ibid.

59. Andrea Boyle Tippett, "Biden Papers Arrive," *UDaily*, June 11, 2012.

60. David Wilson was professor of Political Science and International Relations at UD. He would become dean of the Goldman School of Public Policy at the University of California, Berkeley, in July 2021.

61. The Center for Political Communication and the proposed Biden Institute would be in the new building. It remained undecided which other social science units and programs would be in the building.

62. Ralph Begleiter, email message to author, June 15, 2020.

63. Between 2010 and 2014, CAS undergraduate full-time equivalent (FTE) enrollment as a percentage of total UD enrollment decreased from 45.1 to 40.5 percent. At the same time, CAS externally sponsored activity declined from 26 percent of the university total to 20.3 percent. "CAS Report to Chairs and Directors from Dean George Watson," March 5, 2015. Courtesy of Maria Aristigueta. In the Responsibility-Based Budgeting system, these changes translated into reduced allocated revenue and less opportunity to address the needs of the school and other academic units.

CHAPTER SIX: SHAPING PUBLIC POLICY

1. Thomas Birkland, David Dill, Meredith Newman, Bahira Sherif Trask, Kenneth Wong, "School of Public Policy and Administration Report to Deputy Provost Nancy Brickhouse," October 14, 2014, 1–2. From the author's collection of documents. Unless otherwise noted, primary source materials cited throughout the chapter were obtained from the author's documents.

2. The external review was commissioned by the University Faculty Senate as part of the academic review process for all academic units. See Chapter Five.

3. Birkland, et al., "School of Public Policy and Administration Report," 1–2.

4. State line-item support for programs in the school and its centers decreased from $1,395,600 in 2009 to $1,068,800 in 2013. SUAPP, "Academic Program Review Self-Study," 106–724.

5. Ibid., 107. External funding was $3,915,727 in 2009 and $3,823,730 in 2013. Data through FY20 are from the Biden School transition report "The Biden School's Transition to a Free-Standing Professional School: A Report to the University Faculty Senate," February 10, 2020, 4. Courtesy of the Dean's Office, Biden School of Public Policy and Administration.

6. SUAPP, "Academic Program Review Self-Study," 70–71, and "The Biden School's Transition," 6.

7. The centers provided stipends to sixty-five graduate students each year from 2009 to 2013, at an annual funding level of $750,000. SUAPP, "Academic Program Review Self-Study," 70–71.

8. When Byrne rejoined the school's faculty, CEEP reported to the Dean's Office in the College of Arts and Sciences until the school became a freestanding unit in 2020.

9. Steven Peuquet and Jerome Lewis, "Community Engagement Activities of the

Research and Public Service Units of the School of Public Policy and Administration, College of Arts and Sciences, University of Delaware, July 1, 2011 to June 30, 2012" (unpublished, 2012).

10. The overall impact was to strengthen the nonprofit sector's capacity, particularly benefiting smaller institutions that otherwise would not have had access to professional development opportunities.

11. The Blueprint Communities Delaware program was the first in the nation to include a university component. CCRS provided training, technical assistance, coaching, and financial support to residents to help them develop a strategic plan for their community's future.

12. Data from Christina Morrow, Director, Public Allies Delaware, email message to the author, October 11, 2021.

13. Elizabeth Lockman, quoted by Christina Morrow, email message to the author, October 11, 2021.

14. The work was funded by grants and contracts and informed public policies on such issues as reducing excessive use of emergency room services by better connecting clients to appropriate sources of primary care.

15. Quoted in "Medicaid Research Partnership," *CONNECT* 8, no. 1 (2016): 26.

16. For example, Kathryn Gifford (PhD, UAPP 2016) used Medicaid data for her dissertation and subsequently joined CCRS as a postdoctoral fellow and later as a member of the professional staff to support the expanding research under the new partnership.

17. The center sponsored an area of specialization in the MA in Urban Affairs and Public Policy that later became a graduate certificate program focused on working with faculty and staff on applied projects. In 2010, CHAD proposed a new MA in Historic Preservation, which was offered on a probationary basis but not approved as a separate degree because of resource limitations.

18. CHAD documented two byways—one is in Western Sussex County that lies in the watershed of the Chesapeake Bay, and the second, the Harriet Tubman Underground Railroad Byway, traces the Underground Railroad route through Delaware.

19. Kenneth Becker was president of Becker Capital and Finance. Byrne also worked closely on the development of Delaware's SEU with State Senator Harris McDowell, who described it as one of the great legislative challenges of his long tenure that ultimately gained almost unanimous legislative support.

20. The Better Buildings Challenge is a collaboration of the U.S. Department of Energy and the U.S. Department of Housing and Urban Development to encourage companies and manufacturers, school districts and universities, and state and local governments to adopt efficient building technologies to reduce the wasting of energy.

21. IPA developed online toolboxes of resources that enabled local governments to create comprehensive community plans.

22. The University of Delaware Energy Institute and the Delaware Environmental Institute were both launched at IPA policy forums.

23. Kathleen Murphy also served as associate director of IPA.

24. Gerald Kaufman, "White Paper: U.S. Water and Climate Change Policy" (unpublished, Newark, DE, March 17, 2021), 17.

25. Some of the earliest projects of the Division of Urban Affairs were related to the changing demands on the public education system resulting from shifting demographics and the impacts of federal court-ordered desegregation. Professor Jeffrey Raffel became the chief analyst of the desegregation process. The Center for Applied Demography and Survey Research conducted most of the demographic and enrollment projections for Delaware school districts and conducted periodic surveys on public opinion about

education issues. The Center for Community Research and Service worked with community organizations that provided services to schools and offered supplemental, after-school programs for students and their families. During the period in which the school was a part of CHEP, all of its centers and institutes broadened their engagement on public education issues.

26. The nineteen-member council included early childhood service providers and advocates, state agency representatives, community members, and parents.

27. The adoption of best practices often required additional resources, but state funding of early childhood services was the same regardless of whether those practices were adopted.

28. John Laznick from CADSR was a major contributor to the needs assessment.

29. UD also was one of the only universities in the nation to sponsor an early head start program, New Directions Early Head Start. UD offered direct services through a model Early Learning Center in Newark and an early childhood facility in one of Wilmington's poorest areas.

30. The plan, "Sustaining Early Success: Delaware's Strategic Plan for a Comprehensive Early Childhood System," was developed through a statewide process of engagement, administered by IPA on behalf of DECC, that solicited input from hundreds of families, providers, advocates, and other stakeholders, in addition to early childhood experts and dozens of community partners.

31. Tony Allen spent several years working for U.S. Senator Joseph R. Biden as a speechwriter and special assistant. He became the founding president of the Metropolitan Urban League. He then became executive vice president with MBNA and later communications executive for Bank of America. He was appointed to the University of Delaware Board of Trustees. After serving as provost and executive vice president, on January 1, 2020, Allen became the twelfth president of Delaware State University (DSU). He retained appointments as a senior policy fellow in the Biden School and was a member of the school's Board of Advisors.

32. The website for the commission, subsequently adopted by the Redding Consortium, became the repository for the accumulated research reports, policy briefs, and other analytic resources generated by IPA's staff (www.solutionsfordelawareschools .com).

33. Students were coauthors of all publications, including two books and various policy briefs and reports; some developed their master's and doctoral research around issues of educational equity. Three of the students, Elizabeth Burland (MA, UAPP 2015), Kelsey Mensch (MPA 2018), and Haley Qaissaunee (MPA 2017), were subsequently hired by IPA to continue their work as professional staff.

34. In 2018, a coalition of organizations that included the National Association for the Advancement of Colored People, the American Civil Liberties Union, and Delawareans for Educational Opportunity sued the State of Delaware for failing to provide adequate resources to educate all students effectively. Some of the data and empirical analysis underpinning their claims were based on the research conducted by IPA on behalf of the Wilmington Education Improvement Commission. The main case was settled in fall 2020, leading the state to incorporate funding for low-income students and English learners starting with the FY2022 budget and to make additional adjustments to strengthen support for disadvantaged students.

35. The lead person from Delaware State University was Jason Bourke (PhD, UAPP 2018).

36. SUAPP, "Academic Program Review Self-Study," 3.

37. Ibid., 6–7.

38. The external team included: Thomas Birkland, Professor, School of Public Policy and International Affairs, North Carolina State University; David Dill, Professor of Public Policy, University of North Carolina, Charlotte; Meredith Newman, Professor of Public Administration, Florida International University; and Kenneth Wong, Professor of Educational Policy and Public Policy, Brown University. Dr. Bahira Sherif Trask from the Department of Human Development and Family Studies was appointed by the UD Faculty Senate as the internal member.

39. Birkland, et al., "School of Public Policy and Administration Report," 1–2.

40. "Planning for the Next Generation of SPPA Scholars: A Response to the APR Review Team's Report," School of Public Policy and Administration, November 12, 2014.

CHAPTER SEVEN: RISING EXPECTATIONS

1. He also served as vice president for the Brookhaven National Laboratory. Before joining Stony Brook University, Dr. Assanis had a distinguished career at the University of Michigan for seventeen years. He was the Jon R. and Beverly S. Holt Professor of Engineering and Arthur F. Thurnau Professor, as well as director of the Michigan Memorial Phoenix Energy Institute, founding director of the U.S.-China Clean Energy Research Center for Clean Vehicles, and director of the Walter E. Lay Automotive Laboratory. He also served as the founding director of the interdisciplinary graduate program in automotive engineering (1996–2002), chair of the Department of Mechanical Engineering (2002–2007), director of the Automotive Research Center (2002–2009), and founding codirector of the General Motors-University of Michigan Collaborative Research Laboratory for Advanced Engine Systems (2002–2011). Assanis started his academic career as an assistant and associate professor at the University of Illinois at Urbana-Champaign.

2. His commitment to interdisciplinary inquiry also helped him decide to replace the Responsibility-Based Budgeting system, which he recognized as discouraging interdisciplinary collaborations.

3. Daniel Rich and David Wilson, "White Paper: The Joseph R. Biden, Jr. School of Public Policy and Administration" (unpublished, University of Delaware, June 17, 2016). Obtained from the author's collection of documents. The 2016 white paper was circulated to other members of the UD administration in the fall of 2016. Unless otherwise noted, all primary source documents cited in this chapter are from the author's own collection.

4. Ibid., 1.

5. Ibid.

6. Most national rankings depend primarily on reputational assessments made by the heads of academic programs.

7. The school's faculty subsequently identified four areas for priority in faculty hiring: urban and social policy, health policy and management, energy and environmental policy, and disaster science and management.

8. Quoted in "Biden Institute Announced," *UDaily*, February 7, 2017.

9. Biden also would work at the main Penn campus in Philadelphia.

10. Quoted in Ann Manser, "Biden is Back," *UDaily*, April 7, 2017.

11. Catherine McLaughlin, Biden School website, undated, www.bidenschool.udel.edu.

12. In addition to serving as vice chair of the Biden Institute, she also served as vice chair of the Biden Foundation. The Biden Foundation works to advance issues that Joe Biden and Dr. Jill Biden have worked on throughout their careers, including violence against women, the well-being of military families, equal rights, and affordable education.

13. Quoted in Carlett Spike, "2019 Women of Promise Honored," *UDaily*, March 29, 2019.

14. Rich and Wilson, "White Paper," 2.

15. In 2015, the original task force evolved into the Community Engagement Commission, which studied models and best practices at other institutions to recommend a structure best suited for sustaining and expanding UD's community-based efforts.

16. Maria Aristigueta, email message to author, July 17, 2020.

17. Campus Compact maintained a national posting of the plans submitted. Responsibility for developing the Civic Action Plan rested with CEI.

18. Dennis Assanis, "President's Message," *Civic Action Plan: The University of Delaware's Strategic Vision for Strengthening Community Engagement* (Community Engagement Initiative, December 2017). As the Civic Action Plan was approved, UD joined forty top research universities as part of a subsection of Campus Compact called The Research Universities Community Engagement Network (TRUCEN). The premise underpinning TRUCEN is that one of the measures of every great research university in the twenty-first century is the extent to which the knowledge it generates enriches the quality of life in the communities it serves.

19. The Civic Action Plan presented five overarching goals: enhance university-wide capacity to support community engagement; increase support for engaged scholarship; expand opportunities for undergraduate and graduate students; create new knowledge-based partnerships addressing critical societal challenges; and increase UD's recognition as an engaged research university. CEI was responsible for carrying out the Civic Action Plan. It relied on continuing and substantial support from SPPA to accomplish that task.

20. The Community Engagement Council included representatives from all UD colleges and thirty-seven centers and institutes. In December 2019, Provost Morgan and Executive Vice President John Long created the UD Sustainability Council based on a proposal submitted by CEI leadership and sustainability advocates across campus. The goal was to help align university activities and priorities with its commitment to the environment.

21. The award recipients were Roberta Golinkoff, Unidel H. Rodney Sharp Chair in the School of Education, for her work on early learning, and April Veness, associate professor of geography and Latin American and Iberian studies, for her work with communities in the City of Newark and Sussex County.

22. Kalyn McDonough (PhD, UAPP 2020) from the Biden School received an award for her contributions to the Partnership for Healthy Communities and her work in youth rehabilitation; she also was among the first students to complete the Engaged Scholarship graduate certificate program. In 2021, Biden School doctoral student Dianna Ruberto received an award for her work with the Partnership for Arts and Culture. She also was among the first graduate students to earn a certificate in Engaged Scholarship and taught the introductory course in the Community Engagement Scholars course of study.

23. In 2015, Tony Allen, then a UD trustee, and Dan Rich had encouraged the UD administration to play a more central role in supporting the improvement of Delaware K–12 education.

24. The Partnership for Healthy Communities played a key community support role during the COVID-19 crisis. PHC engaged in forty strategic initiatives to improve the health of Delawareans, including Healthy Communities Delaware, a broad alliance of institutions to support community-led approaches to building healthy and prosperous places.

25. In 2021, Leann Moore (MPA 2014), a professional staff member in the Institute for Public Administration, was appointed TNP's first full-time executive director. TNP also launched the Sustainable Newark Initiative to enhance energy and resource conservation and promote environmental quality practices. The initiative was a partnership between TNP, the City of Newark, the UD Sustainability Council, and business and nonprofit institutions. The TNP received a three-year grant from Chemours to support the Sustainable Newark Initiative.

26. Robin Morgan had been dean of the College of Agriculture and Natural Resources and chair of the Department of Biological Sciences. She joined the UD faculty in 1985 in the Department of Animal and Food Sciences.

27. Overby had been one of the architects of the Civic Action Plan.

28. Quoted in "Joe Biden Calls for Action," *CONNECT* 9, No.1 (2017), 3.

29. Described by Maria Aristigueta, personal communication to the author, November 13, 2019.

30. Papers from the Biden Challenge conference were subsequently published in the *Public Administration Review* 79, No. 5 (September 2019): 621–802.

31. The delay in naming the school was a product of many circumstances. UD had only one named college or school, the Lerner College of Business and Economics, and that naming was accompanied by a sizable endowment. There was no endowment for the naming of the school for Biden. What was never in doubt was Assanis's intention to proceed and make the school's naming a major part of his overall strategy for the university's growth and recognition.

32. Pelesko was appointed as interim dean in September 2018 and then confirmed as the dean by Provost Morgan effective July 1, 2019.

33. Archibald pointed out, for example, that Aristigueta, who held the position of director, was not invited to the periodic meetings of the deans of the leading public affairs schools.

34. The naming of the school was announced without a prior vote of the faculty. Faculty votes endorsing the action were taken in February at the start of the upcoming spring semester.

35. Quoted in Peter Bothum, "New Name, Familiar Face," *UDaily*, December 11, 2018.

36. Ibid.

37. The conversation between Biden and Meacham was preceded by a series of concurrent discussions among policymakers, government officials, business and nonprofit leaders, community members, and UD faculty and students on five areas of importance to the Biden School: American politics and democracy; disaster science and management; energy and the environment; health care; and the middle class and urban affairs.

38. UD was active in politics in other notable ways but without a partisan orientation. For example, the Center for Political Communication sponsored debates among candidates for state office.

39. On February 24, 2019, two months before Biden announced his candidacy, UD Vice President and General Counsel Laure Bachich Ergin circulated a detailed memorandum to the senior administration confirming the legal restrictions on partisan political activities of the university imposed by its charter and by its status as a nonprofit, tax-exempt organization. She wrote that UD is prohibited from participating or intervening in any political campaign or acting on behalf or in opposition to any political candidate.

40. The university's charter expressly forbids the university as an institution from showing favoritism or preference among political parties. The university also required that the Biden Institute's employees and consultants sign an acknowledgment that they understand those policies and would comply with them. The acknowledgement stipulated that "[m]embers of the University community are free to express their political opinions and engage in political activities on their own time and in their private capacity as voting citizens, but they must not do so on university time, using university resources, in such a fashion that the university incurs any expenses, or in a manner that gives the impression that they are speaking or acting on behalf of the university" (Biden Domestic Policy Institute, Political Activity Policy Acknowledgement, UD Office of the Vice President and General Counsel).

41. The 2020 presidential campaign was the first of her brother's political campaigns that Valerie Biden Owens did not lead. While Donilon remained at the Biden Institute during the early period of the campaign, he later moved full-time to Biden's campaign staff.

42. A conservative nonprofit (Judicial Watch) and a news website co-founded by Fox News host Tucker Carlson (Daily Caller News Foundation) called upon the University of Delaware to release the Biden senatorial papers. At the same time, UD was targeted by the Republican National Committee in an ad campaign that chastised the university for not releasing the papers. The call for the release of the papers also came from other media, including *The Washington Post, The Wall Street Journal,* and *The Atlantic.*

43. Biden's explanation for not authorizing the release of the papers was that they did not include personnel documents, such as the ones alleged to exist by the former staff member. If any personnel documents existed, he claimed, they would be in the National Archives. Biden urged the National Archives to release any such documents and requested the U.S. Senate release any records pertaining to the alleged documents. He also indicated that the request to open all the senatorial papers spanning 1973 to 2009 (consisting of 1,800 cartons of papers and 415 gigabytes of electronic records), many of which were not yet curated by the university, would disclose sensitive information, including transcripts of private conversations with world leaders and communications with his staff. Taken out of context, some of this information could damage his campaign.

44. Judicial Watch and the Daily Caller News Foundation filed a combined Notice of Appeal on the opinions of the Office of the Delaware Attorney General.

45. In fall 2021, the Superior Court's decision was appealed to the Delaware State Supreme Court, whose decision is pending as of the writing of this book.

46. Stephanie Feldman, who had served as policy director at the Biden Institute, became deputy assistant to President Biden and senior policy advisor to the director of the Domestic Policy Council. Bruce Reed, who taught as visiting faculty at the institute, was appointed deputy chief of staff. Louisa Terrell, who also taught as a visiting faculty member, became director of the White House Office of Legislative Affairs.

47. Martinez was co-founder and executive director of the Center for Earth, Energy, and Democracy (CEED) in 2011. She helped shape the Equitable and Just Climate Platform in 2018, a collaboration of CEED with the Center for American Progress and the Natural Resources Defense Council that focused on environmental and climate policies. An advocate for environmental justice and efforts to address environmental racism, Martinez championed the rights of Native Americans to have access to clean air and water. Martinez was named one of *TIME Magazine*'s "100 Most Influential People" in 2020.

48. The vote was 34–0 with one abstention.

49. Consistent with Article 3 of the Board of Trustees bylaws, the faculty, ordinarily acting through the University Faculty Senate, had the responsibility to consider and make recommendations for proposed changes in the university's organization. However, the final decision on such changes was with the Board of Trustees, as recommended by the president of the university.

50. There had not been a freestanding school at UD since the trustees determined in 1964 that all the schools at that time would become colleges.

51. The vote was 15–0–8, with the abstentions reflecting on the general issues of university organization and the timetable for action rather than on the substantive merits of the Biden School proposal.

52. Robinson reported that, across the country, university professional programs are typically designated as schools led by deans. These programs offer graduate degrees in such fields as medicine, law, dentistry, public health, architecture, public policy, and education. The accreditation of these programs requires that they be independent units led by an administrator who reports directly to the president or provost.

53. "The Biden School's Transition to a Free-Standing Professional School: A Report to the University Faculty Senate," February 10, 2020, 4. Courtesy of the Dean's Office, Biden School of Public Policy and Administration.

54. The final Senate vote was 53 to 8.

CHAPTER EIGHT: THE BIDEN SCHOOL

1. The two affiliated units had faculty directors with appointments in the Biden School.

2. Sarah Bruch, a sociologist, focuses on the intersections of education and social policy. Gregory Dobler, a physicist, uses techniques from astrophysics to study the dynamics of urban systems that connect people with their natural and built environments. Katie Fitzpatrick, an economist, studies how consumer financial protection, food policy, and health policy can improve well-being. Kimberley Isett, a fellow of the National Academy of Public Administration, studies institutional pressures in delivering services to vulnerable populations. Minion K. C. Morrison, a nationally renowned political science scholar, focuses on comparative politics and administration, racial politics in the Americas, and political leadership. Kalim Shah, a policy analyst, studies sustainable development in island states. A. R. Siders, a lawyer, studies climate change adaptation policies focusing on managed relocation of people and assets away from areas of risk. Daniel L. Smith, an expert in financial management and public administration, studies options to improve financial management in government, health, and nonprofit institutions. Jessica Sowa, a public administration scholar, studies public and nonprofit management issues, emphasizing human resources management in public and nonprofit organizations. Casey Taylor, a public policy scholar, studies natural resources policy and management. Harvey White, a past president of the American Society for Public Administration, focuses on nonprofit leadership, organizational management, and performance evaluation.

3. Danilo Yanich, for example, was conducting research on media and public policy, focused on the influence of money and politics on local television news. See Danilo Yanich, *Buying Reality: Political Ads, Money, and Local Television News* (New York: Fordham University Press, 2020). Another example is Jonathan Justice, a faculty member since 2003, who, together with Daniel Smith strengthened the school's scholarly identity in public budgeting and financial management.

4. Maria Aristigueta, email message to author, July 17, 2020.

5. Karen Stein was director of the Organizational and Community Leadership undergraduate program, 2014–21. Breck Robinson led the Public Policy undergraduate program, 2016–21.

6. In 2019, a new option was approved to enable students majoring in English and minoring in public policy to join the 4+1 master's programs.

7. The conversion of instruction to online formats in a few weeks required a herculean effort. By March 29, 2020, the end of the extended spring break, 6,400 sections of classes were converted to online formats. Before the pandemic, about 3 percent of all UD courses had been offered online.

8. There would be no reduction in the funding of students.

9. Some of the fiscal impacts of the pandemic were later alleviated by the provision of additional federal funding approved early in 2021.

10. The announcement of her appointment was concurrent with the announcement of Louis Rossi as the dean of the Graduate College and Michael Chajes as dean of the Honors College.

11. Isett joined the Biden School in the fall of 2019 after serving on the faculty at Georgia Tech, Columbia University, and Texas A&M.

12. The Biden Institute experienced a 35 percent budget cut and was expected to generate most of its future support from external fundraising.

13. The subsequent restructuring of the Board of Advisors included the appointment of Edward E. (Ted) Kaufman as chair of the board. Kaufman served as Joe Biden's chief of staff during most of his tenure as U.S. Senator. He was appointed to fill out Biden's term as U.S. Senator when Biden became vice president. Sandra Archibald was appointed vice chair of the board. Archibald was emeritus dean of the Evans School at the University of Washington and had been a key advisor during the Biden School's transition.

14. The dialogue was conducted through meetings held on Zoom because of restrictions on in-person campus activities during the pandemic.

15. Aristigueta appointed four co-chairs: Sarah Bruch and Ismat Shah from the faculty, Leann Moore from the professional staff, and Jennifer Daniels, a PhD student.

16. David, an architect and urban planner, was a school faculty member since 2012 and focused her research on land-use planning, growth management, and collaborative governance.

17. The faculty standing committee had been active for decades in supporting the school's leadership role in promoting diversity. Over the previous decade, however, it was less active than it had been earlier.

18. Despite the budget challenges posed by the COVID-19 crisis, President Assanis and Provost Morgan committed start-up funding to support the work of the Anti-Racism Initiative. In October 2020, Assanis took another critical step by appointing Fatimah Conley, who served as Associate General Counsel, as Interim Chief Diversity Officer, reporting directly to him and responsible for overall coordination of DEI efforts.

19. The Biden School proposal was one of many submitted to the university administration for possible inclusion in a funding request to the Unidel Foundation. The Unidel Foundation did provide funding for the university-wide anti-racism initiative, which was designated by the UD administration as a top priority.

20. Notably, the school's faculty had challenged the GRE exam in earlier decades. Those challenges were unsuccessful since the university retained the GRE as a requirement for graduate admission.

21. Quoted in the proposal for Biden Hall prepared by the Office of Development and Alumni Relations, 2021.

22. "Biden Hall Naming Opportunities," Biden School of Public Policy and Administration (unpublished, University of Delaware, December 2020), 1.

23. Quoted in Ann Manser, "Joe Biden & John Kasich, Bridging the Divides," *UDaily*, October 17, 2017.

24. Freel recalls that Biden was "extremely supportive" and that "one session in 2008 lasted for over an hour during which he was asked if they were sitting with the next vice president of the United States. He explained why that was not likely." Ed Freel, email message to author, September 3, 2020.

25. The program gives undergraduate students the opportunity to live in the heart of Washington, DC, for the spring semester while interning in a placement of their choice. The students earn six credit hours for the internship and another six credits for two public affairs classes.

26. Quoted in Chris Kelly, "Delaware Summit on Civics Education," a report posted on the news page of the Biden School website (www.bidenschool.udel.edu), February 7, 2019.

27. Ibid.

28. Timothy Shaffer was appointed as the first Stavros Niarchos Chair of Civil Discourse, effective fall 2022. He was director of civic engagement and deliberative democracy with the National Institute for Civic Discourse at the University of Arizona and served as an associate professor and director of the Institute for Civic Discourse and Democracy at Kansas State University.

29. As a freestanding professional school, the Biden School was able to set its own breadth requirements for undergraduate majors. Previously, those requirements were set by the College of Arts and Sciences.

30. Philip Barnes, email message to the author, September 23, 2021.

CHAPTER NINE: LEGACIES AND POSSIBILITIES

1. Quoted in *School of Public Policy and Administration: 50 Years*, 16.

2. Danilo Yanich, email message to author, June 8, 2020.

3. The long-serving professional staff includes Lisa Moreland Allred, Signe Bell, William Decoursey, Rebecca Gross, Andrew Homsey, John Laznick, Mary Joan McDuffie, Nicole Minni, Troy Mix, Martha Narvaez, Julia O'Hanlon, David Racca, and Kelly Sherretz.

4. Quoted in *School of Public Policy and Administration: 50 Years*, 4.

5. Two good examples are the summer Public Policy Fellows program for undergraduates and the selection of undergraduates as Legislative Fellows.

6. The recipients were Elizabeth Quartararo (2015), Mark Rucci (2015), Linda Halfacre (2017), Zachary Sexton (2018), Nicholas Konzelman (2019), and Bianca Mers (2020).

7. Kristin Fretz and Neil Kirschling, "Government Service is an Honorable Career Aspiration," *The News Journal* [Wilmington, DE], March 15, 2012, 13.

8. Quoted in *School of Public Policy and Administration: 50 Years*, 5.

9. The State's Water Resource Agency is a part of the Institute of Public Administration. The Center for Community Research and Service is the federally approved repository for Delaware Medicaid data and analysis.

10. Quoted in *School of Public Policy and Administration: 50 Years*, 5.

11. Quoted in *Connect* (Newark: School of Public Policy and Administration, University of Delaware, 2016), 16.

12. Quoted in *School of Public Policy and Administration: 50 Years*, 12.

13. The knowledge-based conference series was launched in 2008. The creation of the Delaware Energy Institute was announced at the first knowledge-based partnership conference. The series continued through the next decade and became the public platform for launching the two community engagement partnerships from the 2017 Civic Action Plan, the Partnership for Public Education, and the Partnership for Healthy Communities.

14. Carney's first job in public service came as a member of the inaugural class of the Institute for Public Administration's Legislative Fellows Program. He was secretary of finance under then-governor Thomas Carper. He was twice elected lieutenant governor of Delaware. From 2011 to 2016, he served as Delaware's representative in the United

States House of Representatives. Carney was sworn in as governor of Delaware on January 17, 2017.

15. Lisa Blunt Rochester received her MA in Urban Affairs and Public Policy in 2002. She began her career as a caseworker for then-Congressman (and subsequently Governor and U.S. Senator) Thomas Carper. She served in the cabinets of two Delaware governors as the first African American woman to be secretary of labor, the first African American deputy secretary of health and social services, and state personnel director. She has also served as CEO of the Metropolitan Wilmington Urban League.

16. The Delaware General Assembly includes Senator Elizabeth (Tizzy) Lockman (MA, UAPP 2015), Representative Michael Smith (MPA 2013), Representative David Bentz (MPA 2011), and Representative Madinah Wilson-Anton (MPA 2021).

17. School alumna Jane Vincent (MPA 1995) is a good example. She received her degree as a mid-career student. Vincent continued to collaborate with the school through the next quarter-century while serving as senior vice president for development at the Delaware Community Foundation, regional administrator for the U.S. Department of Housing and Urban Development for the mid-Atlantic states, and president of Delaware Public Media. She continued to teach at the school and collaborate on research and public service projects with CCRS. She also was a member of the school's advisory board.

18. Quoted in "Bold Vision: Biden Institute's Vision to Tackle Nation's Difficult Domestic Problems," March 28, 2017, accessed at the Biden School website, https://www.bidenschool.udel.edu/news/Pages/Biden-Institute-at-UD-Launched.aspx.

19. Biden School Mission Statement, 2021. Obtained from the Biden School website, www.bidenschool.udel.edu.

SELECTED BIBLIOGRAPHY

Barnekov, Timothy K., and Daniel Rich. "Privatism and Urban Development: An Analysis of the Organized Influence of Local Business Elites." *Urban Affairs Quarterly, 12/4* (1977): 431–60.

———. "Beyond Privatism: A Rejoinder." *Urban Affairs Quarterly, 12/4* (1977): 469–75.

Barnekov, Timothy K., Robin Boyle, and Daniel Rich. *Privatism and Urban Policy in Britain and the United States.* New York: Oxford University Press, 1989.

Bebout, John. "Universities and Urban Affairs—Looking Ahead from Back Yonder." *The Social Science Journal 17/2* (1980): 5–19.

Best, Eric, and Daniel Rich. "The Political Economy of Higher Education and Student Debt." In *The Routledge Handbook of the Political Economy of Science,* edited by David Tyfield, 144–55. London: Routledge, 2016.

Best, Joel, and Eric Best. *The Student Loan Mess: How Good Intentions Created a Trillion-Dollar Problem.* Berkeley: University of California Press, 2014.

Biden, Joe. *Promises To Keep: On Life and Politics.* New York: Random House, 2007.

Bok, D. *Universities in the Marketplace: The Commercialization of Higher Education.* Princeton, NJ: Princeton University Press, 2003.

Bourke, Jason. *Urban Governance and Economic Development: An Analysis of the Changing Political Economy of Wilmington, Delaware, 1945–2017.* PhD Diss., University of Delaware, 2018.

Boyer Commission. *Reinventing Undergraduate Education: A Blueprint for America's Research Universities.* New York: Carnegie Foundation for the Advancement of Teaching, 1998.

Boyer, Ernest. *Scholarship Reconsidered: Priorities of the Professoriate.* San Francisco: Jossey Bass, 1997.

Boyer, William W. *Governing Delaware: Policy Problems in the First State.* Newark: University of Delaware Press, 2000.

———, and Edward C. Ratledge. *Pivotal Policies in Delaware.* Newark: University of Delaware Press, 2014.

Florida, R. *The Rise of the Creative Class.* 2nd edition. New York: Basic Books, 2012.

Friedman, T. L. *The World is Flat: A Brief History of the Twenty-First Century.* New York: Farrar, Strauss and Giroux, 2005.

Gavazzi, Stephen M., and E. Gordan Gee. *Land-Grant Universities for the Future: Higher Education for the Public Good.* Baltimore: Johns Hopkins University Press, 2018.

Hoffecker, Carol. *Corporate Capital: Wilmington in the Twentieth Century.* Philadelphia: Temple University Press, 1983.

Horowitz, Irving Louis. "Big Five and Little Five: Measuring Revolutions in Social Science." *Society* (March/April 2006): 9–12.

Irvine, George. *Whither Publicness? The Changing Public Identities of Research Universities.* PhD Diss., University of Delaware, 2018.

Kellogg Commission on the Future of State and Land-Grant Universities (Kellogg Commission). *Returning to Our Roots: The Engaged Institution.* Washington, DC: National Association of State Universities and Land-Grant Colleges, 1999.

Kerr, Clark. *The Uses of the University.* Cambridge, MA: Harvard University Press, 1963.

Kirp, D. *Shakespeare, Einstein, and the Bottom Line: The Marketing of Higher Education.* Cambridge, MA: Harvard University Press, 2003.

Lerner, D. and H. Lasswell. *The Policy Sciences: Recent Developments in Scope and Method.* Stanford, CA: Stanford University Press, 1951.

Munroe, John A. *The University of Delaware: A History*. Newark: University of Delaware Press, 1986.

Newfield, C. *Unmaking the Public University: The Forty-Year Assault on the Middle Class*. Cambridge, MA: Harvard University Press, 2008.

Phelan, J., and R. Pozen. *The Company State: Ralph Nader's Study Group Report on DuPont in Delaware*. New York: Grossman Publishers, 1973.

Raffel, Jeffrey. *The Politics of School Desegregation: The Metropolitan Remedy in Delaware*. Philadelphia: Temple University Press, 1980.

———. *Lessons Learned: A Memoir of Leadership Development*. Washington, DC: NASPAA, 2019.

Rhodes, F. H. T. *The Creation of the Future: The Role of the American University*. Ithaca, NY: Cornell University Press, 2001.

Rich, D. "Academic Leadership and the Restructuring of Higher Education." In *Transitions Between Faculty and Administrative Careers*. Edited by R. Henry, 37–49. San Francisco, CA: Jossey Bass, 2006.

———. "Public Affairs Programs and the Changing Political Economy of Higher Education." *Journal of Public Affairs Education* 19(2) (2013a): 263–83.

———. "The Changing Political Economy of Higher Education: Public Investments and University Strategies." *South African Journal of Public Administration*. 48/3 (September 2013): 429–53.

Rich, D., and R. Warren. "The Intellectual Future of Urban Affairs: Theoretical, Normative and Organizational Options." *The Social Science Journal* 17/2 (1980): 50–66.

Strathman, James G. "A Ranking of US Graduate Programs in Urban Studies and Urban Affairs." *Journal of Urban Affairs* 14/1 (1992): 79–92.

Thelin, J. R. *A History of American Higher Education*. Baltimore: Johns Hopkins University Press, 2004.

U.S. Office of Scientific Research and Development. *Science, The Endless Frontier: A Report to the President*. Washington, DC: U.S. Government Printing Office, 1945.

PHOTO CREDITS

Note: Credits are referenced by figure numbers.

1. © Kathy F. Atkinson/University of Delaware, all rights reserved.
2. Courtesy of the University of Delaware Archives and Records Management.
3. Ron Dubick/USA Today Network, *The News Journal*, April 3, 1968.
4. USA Today Network, *The News Journal*, April 4, 1968.
5. USA Today Network, *The News Journal*, April 5, 1968.
6. Courtesy of the University of Delaware Archives and Records Management, 1980.
7. Courtesy of the University of Delaware Archives and Records Management, 1977.
8. Courtesy of the Delaware State Archives, 1974.
9. Courtesy of the University of Delaware Archives and Records Management, 1978.
10. Courtesy of the University of Delaware Archives and Records Management, undated.
11. Biden School Photo Archives, undated.
12A and 12B. Courtesy of the University of Delaware Archives and Records Management.
13. Courtesy of the Clyde Bishop family.
14A. Biden School Photo Archives, 2013. 14B. Courtesy of Jane Cullingworth, undated.
15. Courtesy of the University of Delaware Archives and Records Management, undated.
16. Biden School Photo Archives.
17. Courtesy of Renosi Mokate and Sibusiso Vil-Nkomo.
18. © Evan Krape/University of Delaware, all rights reserved.
19. Courtesy of the Center for Energy and Environmental Policy, 2014.
20. Courtesy of Melva and Leland Ware.
21. Biden School Photo Archives.
22. Biden School Photo Archives.
23. Biden School Photo Archives, March 21, 2013.
24. © Kathy F. Atkinson/University of Delaware, all rights reserved.
25. Biden School Photo Archives.
26. Biden School Photo Archives.
27. Biden School Photo Archives.
28. Biden School Photo Archives.
29. Biden School Photo Archives.
30A and 30B. Biden School Photo Archives.
31A and 31B. Biden School Photo Archives.
32. Biden School Photo Archives.
33. © Kathy F. Atkinson/University of Delaware, all rights reserved.
34. © University of Delaware, all rights reserved.
35. Biden School Photo Archives.
36. Courtesy of John Byrne and the Seoul Metropolitan Government.
37. © University of Delaware, all rights reserved.
38. Biden School Photo Archives.
39. Biden School Photo Archives.
40. Biden School Photo Archives.
41. Biden School Photo Archives.
42. © Kathy F. Atkinson/University of Delaware, all rights reserved.
43. © Kathy F. Atkinson/University of Delaware, all rights reserved.
44. © Evan Krape/University of Delaware, all rights reserved.
45. © Duane Perry/University of Delaware, all rights reserved.

46. © Kathy F. Atkinson/University of Delaware, all rights reserved.
47. © Kathy F. Atkinson/University of Delaware, all rights reserved.
48. © Kathy F. Atkinson/University of Delaware, all rights reserved.
49. © Kathy F. Atkinson/University of Delaware, all rights reserved.
50. © Evan Krape/University of Delaware, all rights reserved.
51. © Evan Krape/University of Delaware, all rights reserved.
52. © Kathy F. Atkinson/University of Delaware, all rights reserved.
53. © Evan Krape/University of Delaware, all rights reserved.
54. © Kathy F. Atkinson/University of Delaware, all rights reserved.
55A, 55B, and 55C. © University of Delaware, all rights reserved.
56. Biden School Photo Archives, 2015.
57A and 57B. © University of Delaware, all rights reserved.
58. © Kathy F. Atkinson/University of Delaware, all rights reserved.
59A, 59B, and 59C. © University of Delaware, all rights reserved.
60. © Kathy F. Atkinson/University of Delaware, all rights reserved.
61. Biden School Photo Archives.
62. Michael Morris/Biden School.
63. © Kathy F. Atkinson/University of Delaware, all rights reserved.
64. © Kathy F. Atkinson/University of Delaware, all rights reserved.
65. © Evan Krape/University of Delaware, all rights reserved.

INDEX

Printed and bound by CPI Group (UK) Ltd, Croydon, CR0 4YY

16/04/2025

14658333-0003